SO

YOU

WANT

TO BE

PUBLISHED?

by

Róisín Conroy

Attic Press
Dublin

© Róisín Conroy

First Published in Ireland in 1992 by
Attic Press
4 Upper Mount Street
Dublin 2

British Library Cataloguing in Publication Data
Conroy, Róisín
So You Want to be Published? Guide to getting into print
I. Title
070.5

ISBN 1-855940-566

Cover Design: Sinéad Bevan, Attic Press
Origination: Sinéad Bevan, Attic Press
Printing: Guernsey Press Ltd

Contents

For
Gretchen Fitzgerald
without whose friendship and support
this book would not have happened

Acknowledgements

To all my colleagues in Attic Press, Sinéad Bevan, Marie Cotter, Gráinne Healy, Maeve Kneafsey, Orla Pearse, Anne O'Donnell, and Fergus Corcoran, who must take credit for suggesting, insisting and ensuring that this book was written and for all that is best in this work. In addition, Carla King for her flexibility.

To my friends who have given me support when I most needed it, recently, my heartfelt thanks, in particular Pádraigín Ní Murchú, Ursula Barry, Pauline Conroy Jackson, Marianne Henderon, Mary Flanagan, Di Leonard, Lisa Adkins, Gaye Cunningham, Briona McDermott, Ann McDevitt, Patricia Kelleher, Mary Liddy, Colin Conroy, Kate Welsman, Clare Tracey, Freda Roche, Mary Paul Keane, Ellen Kennedy, Rosemary MacMahon and Madgelene Hackett.

For impetus and stimulation my appreciation goes to my colleagues in international world of Women in Publishing (WIP) especially Urvashi, Claire, Brigitte, Clare, Renate, Sue, Araba and Michelle.

I am deeply indebted to Ailbhe Smyth for her indefatigable editing and help with composition of this book. My gratitude also goes to Eleanor Ashe for her guidance, kindness and patience. To them both must also go the credit for all that is best in this work.

My thanks to Michael Gill of Gill & Macmillan for his expert comments and advice on the manuscript.

And in the beginning (Attic October, 1984) .... there was Nell (McCafferty), who on behalf of all authors — had the last word — thanks again.

To my son Joel for his understanding, good humour and love.

About the author

Róisín Conroy, co-founder and Publisher of Attic Press, has been involved in training and publishing for many years. After Róisín studied librarianship and information science at UCD and TCD she spent eight years working as an Information Officer with the Irish Transport & General Workers' Union (now SIPTU); worked as a freelance reporter with RTEs *Women Today* radio programme. In 1982 a constitution case taken on her behalf by Mary Robinson, now President of Ireland, won unemployment assistance for separated women with no child dependants. She has a 19 year old son and lives in Dublin.

Foreword

This book tells you everything you need to know about the world of publishing. It provides clear and straightforward guidelines on how to get your book into print — whether you are a first time writer or a seasoned author.

So You Want To Be Published? details the steps you should take in choosing a suitable publisher, presenting your manuscript or proposal and unravelling the complexities of contracts, agents and royalties. It also outlines the income that you can realistically expect to derive from your writing.

Written from a publisher's viewpoint, it gives an insight into the intricacies and difficulties of publishing which lie behind its 'glamorous' face — both for small specialist presses and larger multinational publishers with several subsidiaries and imprints. Indeed, it is these very intricacies which make publishing such a challenging and fascinating industry.

I have attempted to include all the information I feel will assist a writer through the process of getting published. For this reason the appendices provide a full list of Irish and British publishers and organisations relevant to authors. Also contained are The Minimum Terms Agreement (MTA) with which every writer should be familiar when negotiating a contract and a sample list of awards, bursaries and prizes currently available. Practical information such as the symbols used in proof-reading, how to key in your text and a glossary of publishing terms is also provided.

The initial motivation to write this book came from the wide range of queries we receive in Attic Press on a daily basis, queries which have illustrated to me the many common misconceptions people hold about how the world of publishing works.

At the start of this decade it was predicted that almost everything influencing the success or failure of a publishing house would be radically transformed by the year 2,000 (Henley Consultancy Group). Already, new technology has changed the industry dramatically, as has the control and ownership of the industry. The number of smaller and independent publishing houses has trebled (largely through the advent of Desk Top Publishing). Through mergers and acquisitions some ten companies now control approximately 60 per cent of world publishing. In terms of books published and books in print there have also been enormous changes. Approimately 70,000 *new* books will be published in Ireland and Britain in 1993. The projected figure for the *total* number of books in print in the same year is 700,000. Print runs have, however, decreased and the number of books going out of print each year is rising. The increased competition in the book trade has been quite phenomenal, particularly as book sales have not kept pace with this growth.

As co-founder and publisher of the only feminist press in Ireland, the current statistics on the participation of women in publishing are particularly disturbing.

While women constitute sixty per cent of employees in the publishing industry only two per cent are at the top of their profession internationally, which could explain why the business is commonly referred to as 'the gentlemen's profession'! Most book buyers and readers, throughout the world, are women, yet the majority of books published are written by men (*see Appendix K Reading List* as an example). Although, in terms of books sold, the bestsellers average out evenly between male and female authors.

The power of publishing lies in the *language* of ideas, inspiration, imagination and information which it conveys through the written word. I hope that *So You Want To Be Published?* will help all those who wish to exercise such power. In your endeavours to do so, I wish you good luck.

Róisín Conroy
Autumn, 1992

1 Choosing a Publisher

What kind of publisher?

Publishers invest a lot of time, effort and money in choosing the books they publish. But authors can make choices too! It is very important for you as an author, or a potential author, to choose the right publisher for the type of book you have written or intend to write. You will save yourself a great deal of grief and time if you study the market for your genre and identify possible publishers **before** sending your proposal or manuscript (Ms) out into the deep blue publishing horizon.

Although publishing houses have a good deal in common with one another in the way they are structured and how they work, they tend to specialise in particular areas, for example, children's, poetry, feminist, fiction and non-fiction books. Publishers generally set out to develop a reputation – or 'build a list' – in particular areas and are geared towards reaching specific markets. This means that the 'in house' skills of the staff, their activities, the resources and structure of the house are all reflected in their list(s).

A publisher specialising in a fiction or poetry list will have no interest in an academic text or a book about gardening, while one specialising in children's books will not consider adult fiction or non-fiction books. It is simply a waste of precious writing time, not to mention paper and postage, to send your Ms off to a press that does not publish in your area. In fact, the way you approach a fiction or poetry publisher, for example, is quite different from the sort of approach you would make to a press which specialises in non-fiction.

For a novel, a short story collection or for poetry, the work should be completed, or very near completion, when you make your first contact with a publisher. With non-fiction, you will do better if you present your outline idea with a sample chapter first of all and then, if there is interest in the idea, work with your publisher (or with your agent –

see Chapter 5 for more information) on how best to develop
it, discussing possible angles, market competition and so on.

Most non-fiction books are either commissioned by
publishers or suggested by agents, but this is rarely the case
with fiction and hardly ever with poetry.

Where to find more information about publishers

You should set about choosing your publisher in much the
same way as you would set about finding a home or a
solicitor or applying for a job. First of all, you need to do
your research and find out as much as you can about the
various publishing houses before you take the big jump.
There can be no guarantee of success with your first try, of
course. Knowing where to go will help reduce the number
of rejection slips, which do nothing at all for your self-
confidence and feed the myth that publishers are cold-
blooded monsters who don't care a fig about authors!
Publishers do indeed care about authors — they wouldn't be
in business without them — but no matter how good it is, a
book on teenage health will just not fit into an adult fiction
list and no amount of wishing and pushing will make it do
so.

There are plenty of sources of information about
publishing houses in Ireland and Britain which you can get
hold of with a minimum of outlay and organisation. One of
the simplest things you can do if you live in or near a city or
large town is to have a look in your local library and in
bookshops to get a feel for who is publishing what, and
equally importantly, for what is *not* being published. This
kind of 'look-see-and-feel' exercise is especially useful for
identifying gaps in non-fiction publishing and for seeing
where the 'overload' is in the market. If you have an idea for
a gardening book, for example, you will need to be
confident that it does something very different from the
thirty or so gardening books currently in the bookshops. If
you do discover what appears to be a real gap, you will
want to make sure that you send your proposal in the right
direction as quickly and efficiently as possible.

You, the author, will have to work out who you would
most like to be published by (and why) but you also need to

ask yourself what your book will contribute to 'your' publisher's list! When it comes to proposal or Ms submission time, you are going to have to convince a publisher (or perhaps an agent) that your book is right for them and will enhance their reputation and/or sales.

General trade magazines offer lots of information (as well as trade gossip) on publishing trends and successes and are worth reading from time to time. The most widely circulated magazines are *Books Ireland* (Irl), *The Bookseller* (UK), *Publishing News* (UK) and *Publishers Weekly* (USA). These magazines are heavily used by both publishers and booksellers to help them keep up-to-date with the latest developments and, in the case of booksellers, to guide them in their ordering. From an author's point of view, they give a useful sense of what mainstream publishers are interested in and what booksellers are buying. Apart from all that, they provide a fascinating insight into the marketing and promotional techniques of publishing and especially into the 'hyping' of potential bestsellers and 'bestselling' authors by the bigger mainstream publishers.

As well as the book trade magazines, there are **specialist publications** aimed at confectioners, tobacconists and newsagents (CTNs) and so on. These non-bookshop outlets are important because sales from newsagents and other small shops actually account for around 16 per cent of all books sold, although mainly of the mass market variety. Other specialist 'trade' magazines you may find useful or inspiring include *The Radical Bookseller* (UK), *Books for Your Children* (UK), *Books in the Media* (UK) and *Feminist Bookstore News*(USA). The addresses for many of these publications are listed in the Reading List in *Appendix J*. You could try your local library or make friends with a bookseller to obtain copies of these publications if you don't want to take out a subscription.

The various **writers' directories** also provide key sources of information about publishers. The best known and most reliable directories are the *Writers' and Artists' Yearbook*, *The Writer's Handbook*, Cassell's/PA *Directory of Publishing* and *The Small Press Yearbook*. In Ireland, you could consult *Clé* (Irish Book Publishers' Association). The *IPA* (Institute of

Public Administration) *Annual Yearbook and Diary* gives brief descriptions of each publishing house. Your regional Arts Council office may have more detailed information about local publishers. Names and addresses of a wide range of publishing houses in Ireland and the UK are also listed at the back of this book.

When you have narrowed down your field, write to the various publishers you have identified as most likely to be interested in your work, asking them for a copy of their most recent **catalogue**. Do remember to send a stamped addressed envelope (SAE) to cover postage costs. SAEs are the golden rule of 'unsolicited' correspondence with publishers — without them, you may hear nothing!

A large or small press?

The decision to choose a large, medium-sized or small publisher is entirely up to you. The larger publishing houses have the advantage of big marketing and distribution networks, while small publishers tend to be more specific in the books they publish and target their markets very carefully. Small publishers can also move more quickly than some large ones, which means that, if accepted, your Ms may be transformed into a book sitting gaily on bookshop shelves in a shorter time than it would with a large corporate press. Interestingly, whatever popular mythology may say, your Ms will not necessarily be read and responded to more quickly by a large publishing house. The time-scale for most presses, large or small, is somewhere between three to six months.

Large publishing houses can afford substantial advances (although they almost never pay them to first-time authors) and, if they think your book has real sales potential, they can afford more elaborate promotion. However, with fewer resources, it's clear that small publishers have to work harder at choosing and marketing their books and at developing and nurturing their authors and backlist books. Small publishers simply can't afford to get it wrong if they are to stay in business; they have a much smaller margin of error than the larger presses.

Some authors like the relative anonymity of working

with a large press, while others feel they get more personal attention from a smaller or specialist publisher. It is very important for an author to feel that 'her' publisher and editor are giving her and her book every possible attention. In the end, most published authors agree that a great deal depends on what you, the author, want and what you are most comfortable with. Do you like the 'feel' of a particular press? Do you like the way they market and produce their books? Do you think your book would fit in with the general direction of their list? These are the vital questions, whether you choose a large or a small press. Of course, realistically, on your first outing, it's much more likely that you will be delighted to accept a contract from the publisher who shows immediate interest in your idea or Ms.

One or more submissions at a time?
As a general rule, it is best to make your approach to one publisher at a time. If you do decide to make two or more simultaneous submissions you should say this to each publisher. Processing a Ms and considering a book for publication is an expensive and time-consuming business and quite apart from the ethics of the thing, it is not really in your long-term interest to 'play the field'. There is a strong chance that a publisher will find out that you have made a 'multiple submission', as it is called this may well cause bad feeling and prompt an irritated rejection you might not otherwise have had. A publisher is no keener than anyone else on people who 'play the field'.

If the first publisher has not responded to your submission within, say, three months, write to them asking for a response by a particular date. If at that point you still have heard nothing, you should feel free to submit your proposal or Ms elsewhere.

Different types of publishers
Basically, there are two broad categories of publishing house: **General Publishers** (also known as 'Trade' or 'Consumer' publishers) and **Academic and Specialist Publishers**, for example, poetry, educational/academic, children's, feminist, religious, professional and scientific, technical or medical (STM) publishers.

General publishers

The general publishers are the most visible face of the industry. It is extraordinary that just ten multinational corporations control as much as 60 per cent of British publishing, accounting for a massive chunk of total book sales. These major players, with a sample below of their subsidiary publishing houses and the imprints they own, span not only general but also academic, educational, religious and law books and include:

Bertelsman A G (German) Transworld, Bantam, Doubleday, Corgi, Black Swan, Freeway, Partridge

Reed Elsevier International (Largest UK) Conran, Octopus, George Philip, Mandarin, Heinemann, Butterworth, Hamlyn, Secker & Warburg, Sinclair-Stevenson, Osprey, Minerva, Bowker, Methuen, Routledge, Chapman & Hall, Unwin Hyman, Tavistock, Brimax

Pearson (UK) Longman, Penguin, Viking, Puffin, Pitman, Addison-Wesley, Michael Joseph, Hamish Hamilton, Alan Lane, Signet, Viking, Ladybird and *The Financial Times* (Newspaper)

Random Century (USA) Chatto & Windus, Ebury, Fodor Guides, Bodley Head, Jonathan Cape, Arrow, Red Fox, Vintage, Condé Nast, Hutchinson

News Corporation (Murdoch) HarperCollins, George Allen & Unwin, Grafton, Paladin, Flamingo, Thorsons, Fontana, Times Books, Lions, Mandala, Gower, Basic Books, Pandora, Angus & Robertson Booksellers

International Thomson Sweet & Maxwell, Chapman & Hall, E&J Arnold, Routledge, Croom Helm, Blackie, Nelson

Pan Macmillan (Maxwell) Pergamon, Picador, Sidgwick & Jackson, Harcourt, Brace, Jovanovich (HBJ), Academic Press

Little, Brown and Company (USA) Macdonald, Abacus, Warner-Futura, Optima, Sphere, Orbit

Group de la Cité (France/USA) Chambers, Kingfisher, Millbrook, Grisewood and Dempsey

Hachette/Matra (France)

General publishers are considered to be the high-risk end of the business, because success and failure are almost equally hard to predict in mass markets. Investment in each title is generally high, with print runs often starting at 10,000 and reaching up to hundreds of thousands in the case of bestsellers. Failures are a lot more frequent than most publishers (especially the larger ones) will ever admit, but then rewards from their sometimes unexpected bestsellers can be vast.

General publishers publish both mass-market fiction and non-fiction books aimed at adult 'general readers'. Titles span a huge range of subjects from DIY to travel, biography, crime-fiction, romance and blockbusters. Selected titles are prominently 'hyped' and available 'wherever books are sold' — in large general bookshops and chains like WH Smith (who own Waterstones), Eason's, Books Etc., Book Centres, Dillon's, as well as in newsagents, hotels, airports and so on.

Traditionally, general publishers were divided into the 'Hardback' houses producing original (new) books and the mass-market 'Paperback' houses which bought the paperback rights to the hardback titles. Over the last few years this has changed, along with a good deal more in the business. There have been so many 'take-overs' and 'mergers' that the long-established distinctions between Hardback and Paperback houses have now all but disappeared.

Unlike other publishers, the general trade paperback houses have been steadily increasing the number of 'original' (new) books they publish each year, which may seem like good news for authors. But — and it's a very big but — they are so deluged with manuscripts that it is extremely difficult for a first-time author to succeed in having her Ms accepted by one of these large publishing houses. Each year they reject on average 97 per cent of the manuscripts which swamp their editors' desks. Collins, for instance, receive a total of 5,000 unsolicited Mss per annum, 99 per cent of which never make it past the first reader. However depressing it may be for authors to hear, it's a fact that most general publishers' books are specially commissioned.

Academic and **Specialist Publishers** cover a wide variety of presses. They publish in more specific areas for a more closely defined readership. These houses are far more likely to be 'independent', ie not owned by multinational companies, and tend to be run by an individual or a small group of individuals with a particular interest or expertise in the publishing house's subject specialisation. The smaller and independent specialist presses are ever-wary of having their strongest selling authors 'poached' by the bigger houses – lured away from them by the promise (not always fulfilled!) of fatter advances, bigger hype and richer sales.

Of course, the general and specialist categories are by no means watertight. There is a fair degree of overlap in the kinds of books published by both types of press.

As publishing has changed over the past few years – and many of the changes have been little short of dramatic – it has become increasingly difficult for the more successful of the independent publishers to resist take-overs by the bigger companies. Independent, specialist and smaller publishers are becoming something of a rarity in the increasingly 'multinationalised' world of books.

However, the pressure on the smaller and independent presses has had some positive spin-off. Many of them have held off take-overs by developing broader and more popular lists. The range of areas covered by many of these presses is now more diverse with, for example, women's presses producing books for teenagers, science fiction, detective novels and so on.

Literary Fiction

Some presses have built up especially strong lists of high-quality serious fiction. Many publish only in hardback and 'sell-on' the paperback rights to another publisher, while others do both hardback and paperback. Increasingly, the trend is for novels to be published as 'paperback originals' as readers become more resistant to paying high prices for a hardback book which, if successful, will appear in paperback within a mere six months.

There is of course no point in sending a romantic novel or horror story to a 'literary' press. While the bigger houses are more likely to consider Mss through a reputable agent, their editors also keep a very sharp eye on the 'literary scene' and are interested in seeing the work of writers who are just beginning to establish a name for themselves. Most literary presses, through their editors, tend to nurture their authors very carefully and dread the thought of having them poached by rivals! Of course, if you feel yourself being 'poached', this could be a clear sign that you are making some kind of impact even though the royalties on your first book may be dismally low. It is also, less pleasantly, possible that you are being used as a 'carrot' in order to attract other authors whom the publisher really wants in order to build a list. British publishers have been known to do this with Irish authors. You should not assume, by the way, if a large publishing house wants your novel, that they will necessarily pay you a very large advance. (It is another myth, put out by rivals, that most smaller publishing houses do not pay the same advances or royalties as large houses.) Advances are closely based on predicted sales figures and the vast majority of serious novels do not achieve the level of sales necessary in order to translate into real money for their authors. However prestigious the house, print runs of 1,000 or 1,500 are not at all unusual for serious fiction, and especially for first-time authors.

Short stories

Most of what I have just outlined about literary fiction also applies to short stories. Generally speaking houses focussing on literary fiction publish some short story collections, as do many specialist presses. But short story collections very rarely sell as well as novels and this means that publishers are much more reluctant to accept them. On the whole, you are unlikely to place your short stories with a large general publisher unless you are an Ursula K LeGuin.

Poetry

Poets tend to believe that poetry is by far the most difficult kind of writing to get published. This is not entirely accurate. There are many excellent poetry presses and you should consult the *Writers' & Artists' Yearbook*, *The Writer's Handbook* and *Small Press Yearbook* for a listing. In Ireland, for example, there are Gallery, Salmon, Beaver Row, Dedalus and Blackstaff. In England mainstream houses which publish poetry include Faber, OUP, Chatto, Secker, Deutsch,

Methuen, Polygon and there are the specialist Onlywomen, Gaymen's Press, Bloodaxe, Carcarnet, Seren and Sheba presses, for example. If you have managed to establish some sort of reputation for your work in poetry magazines, it probably stands a higher chance of being published than a collection of short stories or experimental fiction (which most British and Irish publishers tend to avoid). What is absolutely true is that poets rarely earn much money from their books. But then, you hardly need this book to tell you that!

When sending a sample of your poems (six or seven should be enough), do include a list of all the publications (magazines, journals, newspapers, etc) in which your poems have appeared. Magazines which publish poetry include *Poetry World, Poetry Review, Literary Review, London Review of Books, Times Literary Supplement (TLS), Krino, Cyphers, Honest Ulsterman,* and *Poetry Review.*

Plays

Whatever poets and short story writers may say, playwrights have most difficulty being published. The chances of seeing your play in print are slim even if it has been produced with some success. Those chances can dwindle to zero if you have not had your play performed. So be warned! Still, Methuen, the UK publishers, specialise in this area, if you are feeling brave and persistent. It is best on the whole to have an agent, if you can find one to take you on.

Non-fiction

Non-fiction obviously covers a huge range of possible topics, which I cannot go through in detail here. My general advice, to choose your publisher carefully, is especially important with non-fiction. Depending on your subject, you may choose either a general or a specialist press. Work out who seems to be publishing the most, or the most interesting books, in your area. Ask yourself if your book (or idea) links in well with other books or series a publisher is doing. See if your idea fills a gap in their list. The more original your idea and your treatment of it, the more likely it is to be considered.

Feminist (women's) presses

The feminist presses which have blossomed in Ireland and Britain over the past twenty years have their roots in the women's movement. Often fiercely resisted in the early years by the mainstream publishers, the book trade and the literary establishment, the pioneering feminist publishing houses persisted and demonstrated beyond all shadow of doubt that there is an ever-growing and very diverse market for exciting work by women writers. The feminist presses have not only introduced fine new women writers to readers, but provided the legitimate space for women from different backgrounds and cultures to write about their experiences and perspectives.

Over the years, some feminist presses have developed large and varied lists, while others have chosen to remain small or medium-sized, providing ground-breaking space for ideas and perspectives dismissed by 'mainstream' publishers as too 'risky'. Of course, when the 'risky' books sell (which they frequently do), the mainstream tends to get very interested indeed. There is nothing like ££ signs for bringing the light of understanding to publishers' eyes! Most feminist presses publish a wide range of books, both fiction and non-fiction. In Ireland there is Attic Press and in Britain Onlywomen, Scarlet Press, Sheba Feminist Press, Open Letters, The Women's Press and Virago. Although there are considerable differences between them, they are, in a sense, general publishers with a specialist interest — women's issues. Some include a political (small 'p') dimension to their lists; others may place an emphasis on feminist 'classics', both fiction and non-fiction, or lesbian or black women's experience and literature and poetry; some publish more fiction than non-fiction or vice versa.

Children's presses

Children's publishing spans a wide age and interest range, from babies to teenagers, and includes board books, picture books, annuals, fiction, highly-illustrated information books and project-based material for classroom use. These books account for over one in five of all books sold in Ireland and Britain, and are published by divisions of some general publishers and by specialist children's presses. The text and illustration of children's books must appeal to the children who read them and the adults (parents, teachers, relations, librarians) who buy, or influence children's and teenagers' choice of books. Writing for younger children is a highly specialist activity and most books for younger children are illustrated. Given its breadth and diversity, it is not an easy market to cater for and is notoriously difficult to break into for first-time authors. As in a number of other areas, and especially if you are looking towards the larger publishers, you probably have a better chance of having your Ms considered if it is recommended by an agent with a track record in the area. The number of presses who publish books for children and teenagers in Ireland and Britain is too long to list here. I suggest you consult the list of Irish publishers in *Appendix A* and *The Writers' and Artists' Yearbook* which classifies publishers by subject.

Educational and text book publishers
Books used in schools and colleges are nearly always written by teachers or by people with teaching experience. The books are tailored to particular syllabi and to quite specific age groups. Making early contact with the publisher is vital, as you will be closely assessed to determine your ability to write for a particular level.

The best way to break into this most difficult area is to find a new approach to a well-tried subject. The publisher will not make a final decision on your proposal without first researching how widely the subject is taught, how much syllabus time is given to it and, of course, whether teachers will actually use the book.

Illustrations, which are expensive, often form an important part of a school book.

Academic and University presses
Academic and University presses publish research-based, scholarly and theoretical work in the academic 'disciplines'. Some are highly specialised, focussing on, for example, the very lucrative scientific, technical and medical (STM) textbook market or areas within the humanities or the social sciences. Academics usually choose their own topic for

research, and discover through word of mouth which publishers are most likely to have an interest in their work. Because of the 'publish or perish' principle that operates in the academic world, authors often behave as if their publisher were doing them a service, even a favour, in publishing their Ms. They tend to pay far too little attention to the terms of their contract, to advances or to potential royalty earnings since what is most important to them is getting their name known.

Print-runs on academic books are often surprisingly small and so the retail price of the book can be very high.

Reference book publishers

Reference books rarely result from proposals from potential authors and are mostly commissioned by the publishers. They are often the work of a large and carefully organised team of contributors, working to the brief of a small board of specialist editors. One person usually acts as the overall guiding editor, ensuring an even balance between the different areas of the book, with a specialist section editor for each individual area. Section editors usually work to a very strict timetable with detailed guide-lines to ensure consistency.

Book packagers

Packagers literally put a 'book package' together and then pre-sell it to various publishers around the world. They concentrate on books that are expensive to produce with a broad international appeal or a formula which can be adjusted slightly for several markets, for example, art and photography books. 'Book packages' are often the work of two or more authors. A once-off fee payment, rather than royalties, is the norm. Authors tend to be approached by packagers rather than the other way round, and in fact most book packagers work almost exclusively with agents.

Self publishing or DIY publishing

This is not to be confused with Vanity Publishing! Gertrude Stein, Virginia Woolf, Anais Nin and many more published their own work at some time in their lives. If you feel you have the time, patience and the all-crucial business skills, there is no reason why you can't learn about the publishing and design process yourself (see *Glossary* for details of terms used), and publish your own book!

First of all, get plenty of concrete ideas by having a close look at how other books are produced. Then set about getting quotations (estimates) from printers and also from typesetters if you are not using your own Desk Top Publishing (DTP) system. You may want to have the cover professionally designed, so you will need to contact designers (use the *Writers' & Artists' Yearbook*, *The Writer's Handbook*, *Small Press Yearbook* or *Golden/Yellow Pages* for listings).

It is absolutely vital to cost the whole business before you get embroiled with designers, printers and all the rest of the complicated business of book publishing. Be realistic; if it's going to cost more than you can possibly afford and/or more than you can expect to get back in sales, **abandon** the project and continue sending your proposal to publishers!

The cost of publishing a book depends on the number of pages and the number of copies of the book or pamphlet you want to print. It can range from a couple of hundred pounds to over £5,000 — and more. A very simple way of working out the cost per book is to divide the **total costs** (design, setting, printing and so on) by the number of books you want to print.

For example, if the total cost of setting, designing and printing a 128 page book is £2,000 and you intend printing 500 copies, the unit cost will be £4 (a 'unit' is what publishers rather callously call a book in cost terms!).

Then you need to work out the selling price of the book. Your retail price must take into account the discount you will have to give each seller (bookshop or other sales outlet) for selling the book for you, plus the cost of getting the book to them (distribution) and the cost of getting your money back. You should also include advertising costs if that's going to help you reach more readers. So, if each book costs £4.00 to produce, you will have to sell it at a minimum of £10 in order to give the seller a cut and in order for you to recoup your basic costs, with no profit. The next question, of course, is how many people will pay £10 for your 128 page book? Research your market thoroughly before you make any decisions about print numbers.

Many authors give up or become frustrated because of the amount of unexpected work and money involved in the process of self-publishing. Get as much advice as you can and don't print high numbers in order to cover costs. It is difficult to DIY — but not impossible!

Of course, publishing your own book on a once-off basis is one thing; setting up a small press is quite another matter. But, if you have a little capital, some specialist advice and access to a desk-top publishing (DTP) system (computer, good software programme and laser printer), and a gambler's temperament (or a lot of nerve) you can become a publisher of books, magazines or pamphlets. DTP has been responsible, in part, for the emergence of about 6,000 small presses in the UK and it has been estimated that there will be around 200,000 small presses in the USA by the end of the decade. DTP has attracted discontented authors who have been turned down by publishing houses and agents as well as publishers who have ceased working for the big houses. DTP has also been responsible for the recent massive increase in books, some bizarre and outrageous, others satisfying readers who are bored with much of the orthodox literature. Still, despite the technological advances, one of the biggest, and oldest, problems for many of these small presses is getting their books distributed and reviewed.

Local and community publishing

With the inception in 1972 of the Centerprise publishing project in Hackney, London and the KLEAR (Kilbarrack Local Education for Adult Renewal) Group in Dublin in the early 1980s there has been a slow but steady growth in local community publishing. Many of the books published by these groups originate in writers' workshops and writing groups. They cover collections of prose or poetry, local histories, or autobiographies of working class people. Each group has their own particular way of selling their own publication. Some groups tend to rely on their local shops to sell the books while other groups refuse to sell through shops, preferring to operate door to door, face to face. Books are also sold at meetings, in pubs, at readings, on trains, in bulk orders to local schools and by any other means possible. You should contact your local library, bookshop, trade union, Workers' Education Association (WEA), Federation of Worker Writers and Community Publishers, VEC or consult a list of adult training courses, guides to evening classes and *The Attic Guidebook & Diary* to make contact with a group in your area.

Vanity publishing

If a book is worth publishing the costs should be borne by a publisher or you should control everything yourself. You should *never* pay anybody else to do it for you. Publishers and authors' organisations constantly warn against the dangers of vanity publishing. In their efforts to get business vanity publishers advertise widely. In the guise of scouting for new talent in the areas of short fiction, autobiography and poetry (the most difficult areas to sell), vanity publishers send back exaggerated reports of praise to authors and raise hopes of commercial success by promising high sales, of say, 2,000 plus copies of your book.

They then ask the author to 'invest' or to pay a fee, explaining that this is a commercial risk which they cannot bear alone. In fact, vanity publishers rarely print more than 200 copies of any book. You are of course entitled to pay for the publication of your work but you are strongly advised not to. If your Ms is worth publishing, a reputable publisher will do it at her own expense. If you cannot get your Ms accepted by a reputable publisher and you absolutely must see it in print, do it yourself!

2 How Publishing Works

The publishing business

By business standards, book publishing is a relatively small but influential industry. Between Ireland and Britain there are about 14,000 active publishers, which includes many small presses and those for whom publishing is a sideline. However, recent mergers and the disappearance of some presses have narrowed the range of choice for authors. Two handfuls of very large multinational publishing groups now control well over half the world market, and several of these companies are involved in newspaper, television, magazine, bookshops, printing and other (often unrelated) interests.

The on-going war of publishing mergers (which seems to be mainly between large American, German, French and British houses) means that owners, and therefore bosses, can change overnight. This is not an easy situation for people working in the business. It also has a negative impact on authors when editors, with whom they may have built up a close working relationship over a number of years, are suddenly switched to a new imprint, lose their jobs or decide not to stay on with the new owners. Overall, the 1990s are a rather uneasy period for publishers and the industry as a whole.

How publishers choose their books

There are several interrelated factors which can influence a press's decision to publish a book.

Suitability for the list. A book has to fit the style and aims of the list for which the house is known so that it is compatible with the press's particular markets. Editors must keep in mind the list's overall balance, direction and originality when making their decisions.

Content. The initial proposal to the publisher or editorial board is based on the editor's judgement of the quality and appropriateness of the Ms. Fiction editors may use sub-editors or external readers to offer first and/or second opinions. Non-fiction editors may ask specialist external readers to comment on specialist titles. Specialist and academic publishers rely heavily on experts (academics, professionals), sometimes world-wide, to comment on material initially, during and/or after the book has been written. All these readers are paid small fees and remain anonymous to the author.

Author assessment. The author's skills, qualifications, motivation and time available to write the book will all be elements in the publisher's (or editor's) decision. The author's ability to deliver on time, to help promote the book, and her responsiveness to editorial suggestions are all very real factors in deciding whether or not to go ahead.

Market. The main audience for which the book is intended, who will buy it, the possible sales on home and overseas markets are key factors. Indeed, editors in the larger houses say that publishing decisions are basically made by the sales and marketing directors. Editors provide the material (ie the ideas and the proposals), but the money men make the decisions. Good editors often have to fight very hard for books they believe in, and most of them do, luckily for authors and readers. The sales performance on the author's previous books or on similar books may be used as a guideline. The rights sales potential is usually assessed (book club, USA rights) as well as special marketing opportunities on which the book could be promoted.

Competition. The book's main selling points and its advantages compared with the publisher's existing backlist titles and competitors' books are all taken into consideration. This applies mainly, of course, to non-fiction.

Format and price. The book's physical appearance (length in words, illustration, content, binding style and production quality), the likely cost and price range into which it would be sold are very important elements in this process.
Apart from the editor or editorial department, it's obvious

that a lot of people have a say in whether or not a book should go ahead. The sales and marketing people are involved in pricing and sales forecasts. The production people work on costs. A reader's profile is prepared (covering the scope of book, market and competition, publication dates, reasons for publication and so on). A financial statement sets the expected sales revenue against the cost of producing the book and the author's royalties to give the hoped-for profit margin, provided the book sells out.

Some ideas are rejected immediately as unsuitable, others after one or two reader's reports. Some authors are asked to re-submit in the light of editors' suggestions others are followed up and get the go-head and at this stage the contract with the author or agent is negotiated. Of course, an author may still have considerable re-writing to do even after the contract is signed, but it is at least on the basis of a firm commitment.

What happens to your proposal or manuscript?

Your proposal (and or sample chapters) arrives on a desk in the editorial department. It is logged in, acknowledged, and will usually be given a brief glance immediately. It will then be sent in one of several possible directions. It can be (a) rejected as unsuitable for the list, (b) passed to an in-house/external specialist reader, (c) possibly read by the editor (or series editor) herself before making a further decision.

Most editors are under considerable pressure to produce books and to do so profitably. This inevitably means that authors with a good track record are likely to get more immediate attention than those publishing their first book. A team of people both inside and outside the house will frequently be called upon for specialist advice and skills. You should not feel at all slighted if your Ms is given to an outside reader. This is normal practice. You can take comfort from the fact that, following your proposal, you have actually been asked for the Ms and that if it is sent for reading it is usually read twice, if not three times, before a final decision is taken.

Readers are 'weeders' (we're talking about publishers' readers here, not book-buyer readers!) and are expected to know something about the market, or the potential market, for your book and to be able to distinguish between good and bad writing. An important qualification is that the editor can rely on the judgement, or 'nose' as it is called, of her readers. The reader's report provides a detailed summary of the book's contents as well as the reader's recommendation and sometimes confirms a judgement already made in the publishing house. The reader's report will be carefully studied by the editor. If the editor is still unclear or undecided she will look for another opinion.

Even if the reader's report is favourable, the house may not yet be ready to move to the next stage, ie the preparation of an estimate. The reader or editor may decide that the book requires additional work or even re-writing before it can be accepted. In this case the editor will usually invite the author to come in and talk about it. Good editors can contribute enormously to the improvement of a book.

Every editor has a pile, mountain high, of unsolicited Mss which must be read. It is no secret that 99 per cent of these will be rejected as unsuitable but they will all be gone through because a good editor just cannot afford to miss the gem that might lie there. Although the publisher is in a buyer's market, the number of books that come in unsolicited, and end up on the bestseller lists is very small indeed. Most either do not suit the list or are not well written. Of course publishers make mistakes and reject books that come back to haunt them for ever more, but the system is designed to try and minimise this by spreading the decision-making load.

If the editorial reports are favourable and the author agrees to do the suggested rewrites, the book will then be assessed by the finance department, and the cost of manufacture, print quantity, potential sales and income will be estimated. Subsidiary rights income (*see Glossary and chapter 6 on Contracts & Royalties*) will also be worked out. The finance department may discover that the sales potential and profit margin are too low. This will be discussed at an editorial meeting where adjustments may be suggested such as reducing the number of pages (extent) or the number of illustrations, increasing the price or adding markets for sales. A number of estimates may have to be prepared before the right formula is found. It can be at this stage that the editor has to reluctantly reject the book, basically for financial reasons. The process can be very time consuming and partly explains why authors have to wait so long for a final decision. There is no guarantee of acceptance until the publisher is ready to discuss a contract with an author.

Once the contract is signed, your Ms then goes into production, and this process can take anything between three to twelve or even eighteen months. On the whole, bigger publishers tend to have a much longer 'turn around' period for production. Smaller presses move more quickly because they simply cannot afford to tie up their resources for such a long time.

First of all, the editorial people check the Ms to ensure that the content, style and so on is in accordance with the agreement. Suggestions for developments and improvements may be made at this stage, which means more author rewrites!

When the text comes back it is thoroughly checked, first by the editor, and then in detail by a copy-editor for completeness, consistency, house style, libels and to ensure that all copyright matter has the necessary permissions. Any queries are checked with the author.

When the design process has been completed and the camera ready copy (CRC) prepared (more about all of this later!), your book goes to the printers. When they have done their job, copies are delivered to the publisher's warehouse where it stays for a minimum of ten days (or until five days before publication date) when it is released to the book trade. Advance copies (sometimes called 'finished copy') of the book usually arrive from the printer about three weeks before publication and are sent out as 'review copies' to the relevant media. For maximum publicity impact, the publication date is usually set some weeks after the delivery of bound copies. This means bookshops can get their stock in time and reviews or advertising will have begun to appear.

Publication date

Publishers want to sell the maximum number of books so they will choose the most suitable time to publish each title on their list. It is in their own interest as well as the author's to do this. Some books, for instance, are brought out in time for Christmas, others as 'summer reading' or perhaps to coincide with a particular event.

Publication day

It can take up to nine months and longer for a book to go through the complicated publishing process. Of course, by publication day, all the work has already been done. So, although it's a significant and very happy day for *you*, in a sense it's just another day in your publisher's life. Still, most publishers know how important a day it is for the author, and you can expect lunch or at least some flowers to celebrate!

After publication

From the author's point of view, very little seems to happen after your book has been published. Somehow, it seems like a big let-down after all the hard work. Reviews rarely appear on publication day and of course many books are never reviewed at all. In fact, the sales people are continuing to actively sell your book which has now become part of the press's backlist. This may seem harsh, but it's reality! Your editor or agent's efforts on rights sales may go on for quite some time, especially if the book is well reviewed or is arousing interest generally. The marketing department will keep you informed of any news on the media front. You will then have to wait until the royalty statement appears to learn the full truth. Try to resist phoning your publisher or editor everyday for 'news'. If there is any, believe me, you'll get it. If you contact your publisher too often you become a public nuisance.

What publishers do

Publishing a book is a complex business which involves many different processes and stages and a wide range of skills. Knowing exactly how publishing works and what goes on inside a press will give you a better sense of control when you are dealing with your publishing house.

A publishing house is usually divided into a number of areas or departments, including Editorial, Design and Production, Sales and Marketing, Finance and Distribution.

Main functions in a publishing house

Editorial may consist of (a) commissioning and sponsoring editors or editorial consultants, (b) desk or managing editors and (c) rights and permissions editors. Depending on the size of the house, the list may be divided up, with separate editors for, say, fiction and non-fiction or for different series. Within fiction there may well be specialist editors for children's, teenage, or adult fiction for example. Many publishing houses also have an editorial board which makes the final decisions about publications.

The commissioning editors, working on their knowledge of the market and specialist areas, decide which books or projects should be commissioned and which manuscripts should be accepted or rejected. They are constantly researching and building up contacts in their specialist areas.

The desk or managing editor takes responsibility for the day to day management of the list which can include reading, editing, proofing and copy-editing, assessing quality of authors' work, overseeing the work of copy-editors, readers and proof-readers, scheduling and monitoring production and of course liaising with authors.

Rights/permissions editor or manager: Literary agents often handle the prime publishing rights on behalf of the author they represent. However, many authors do not employ agents and the sale of subsidiary rights are often dealt with by specialist staff within publishing houses. In smaller publishing houses the task of negotiating and selling rights may lie with the publisher and marketing or editorial staff. The range and financial significance of different rights for sale in the publishing process has expanded over the years.

The role of the staff is to assess and promote the different rights' potential, locate likely buyers, and negotiate the best possible terms.

The copy-editor's task is to check the text in detail for consistency, accuracy and completeness. She corrects any errors of content or of style, for example, checking literals (errors such as spelling mistakes), indentation of paragraphs, italicisations, facts, inconsistencies, and, where necessary, rewriting phrases or sentences.

The corrected Ms is returned to the author for approval and then, on its return, is sent to production who include any changes in the final copy.

Proof-readers: While authors are normally asked to proof-read the text of their book, it will also be proofed 'in house' by at least two proof-readers. Corrections and changes are put together by the editor (or)desk editor. After the final proofing and editorial checking, camera ready copy (CRC) is passed for press (printing).

Design: Once your Ms has been accepted a designer is commissioned to design the cover. The designer usually works closely with the marketing, editorial and production departments. Book design is a highly skilled specialist area and the designer is a very important person in the publishing business (although not necessarily highly paid). The *look* of a book is crucial to how it will sell and with intense competition for shelf space in bookshops, design has become increasingly important.

The production department transforms the copy-edited and proofed texts into printed books. The production manager works with designers, printers, paper merchants and binders and decides the finer details of type, number of pages, chapter openings, number of illustrations and their position. Each book gets individual treatment: format, page layout, typeface, typesize and paper need to be chosen, a binding selected and cover design commissioned, all within a predetermined budget.

By the time the final corrections are entered into the text, a decision on the print quantity and printer will have been taken. The production department passes the order to the printers and monitors the book's progress through all stages up to delivery.

The final number of copies to be printed is decided on the basis of advance orders (subs) and market knowledge. Up to now the sales and marketing people have been using the cover and advance information on the book to sell it. While the book is printing the sales and marketing people will be working on increasing the sales figures and on media coverage.

The sales, marketing and publicity departments play a crucial role in shaping a publisher's list, ie in the decision to accept or reject a book. They also report on market trends, suggest specific titles or topics for publication to the editors, together with forecasting and budgeting. It's difficult to totally separate the work of these three areas since so many of their tasks overlap.

As soon as a new book is given a tentative publication date, or sometimes even when it is first signed up, the sales department informs the wide international network of sales reps and agents, giving as many details about the book as possible, and the selling of that book begins. Distributors, wholesalers, library suppliers, overseas outlets all have to be informed, persuaded and encouraged to order each new book.

The sales representatives (Reps) will call on the bigger customers several times, normally with a list of forthcoming books. It is the reps, with their knowledge of the customer and their own reputation and that of the house, who also convince the book buyer to re-order books from the publisher's backlist.

The most common sales aids used by reps are the jackets/covers/flyers, catalogue and advance information sheets (AIs). Few of the sales that the rep makes immediately are 'firm'. Almost all are 'on sale or return', meaning that the bookseller can return the books, after a reasonable period, if they fail to sell.

Advertising: Most publishers believe that advertising in the national press is a waste of money and only satisfies the author's ego. There are other more effective ways of publicising a book, through reviews, for example, and of course radio and TV. The vast majority of people who buy or read books do so because they have heard about them through word of mouth or because they see a book displayed in a shop, like the look of it and buy it on impulse. Booksellers' recommendations are also very influential and reviews can be persuasive with certain kinds of books. Publishers tend to concentrate on the booksellers, aiming a good deal of their advertising at them because, after all, if the book is not in the shops and prominently displayed, no one is going to be able to buy it. Advertising is placed in key trade periodicals such as *'The Bookseller' 'Publishing News' 'Books Ireland'* and key specialist magazines read by booksellers and librarians.

The marketing department produces a catalogue of the press's titles, with a blurb (short description of the book) and sometimes an illustration of the book or photo of the author. The catalogue includes the publication date, price and various other important trade details. This is sent to the trade and potential buyers of rights and to key members of the public who are on the publisher's mailing list.

The main task of the marketing and publicity department is to promote and publicise new books. Promoting the backlist comes second to this. They usually write the catalogue inserts and cover blurbs, issue press releases and other publicity information. It's also their job to organise advertising (which may be contracted out to a separate agency), to decide who will get review copies and to raise and follow up on media interest by arranging author interviews, book signings, author tours, exhibitions, speaking events and so on.

It's in the area of publicity and promotion that authors tend to be most critical of their publisher and where some authors feel that their publisher has failed them dismally. However, most publishers, large or small, have a publicity budget and each book gets a share of this, in proportion to its expected sales. Authors do have to remember that theirs is not the only book being published in a particular season — no book can have the entire budget and publicity department energy all to itself! Most presses ask authors to fill in a publicity questionnaire, usually when the contract is being signed.

Proof and review copies of books are sent out to the relevant media. Depending on the type of book, copies may be sent to the major national and provincial newspapers, magazines, specialist publications, radio and TV programmes and key people in relevant organisations. The publicity people will use favourable quotes from reviews in advertisements and on the cover of the book if it is reprinted.

A lot of energy goes into trying to get radio and television interviews for the author. Tours are exhausting and they usually involve signing sessions which most publishers and booksellers dislike. If crowds flock to the bookshop, this is wonderful, of course. But if not, a signing can be the most dismal and depressing non-event for both the author and her publisher.

The **launch** used to be a regular feature of publishing life but is now much less common. Many an author offering to pay for the launch of her own book has been refused on the basis of cost effectiveness. The people who turn up at launches are generally the author's family and friends, the publishing staff and the very occasional journalist or bookseller.

While publicising books is part of the publisher's role, a lot can depend on the author too! She can do a great deal to 'sell' her book by being positive in interviews (and available), and by making sure that what she has to say is stimulating, interesting and well thought out.

International book fairs: Book fairs form an important part of the publishing scene. They are held in many countries throughout the world. Book fairs provide opportunities for the sale and purchase of rights and for booksellers to order books. Many publishers feel that it is essential to attend these events and often spend a considerable amount of money travelling there, hiring a stand to display their books and on hospitality for their customers. Other publishers stay away from them. The atmosphere at many of these fairs is hot, noisy, and busy.

Probably the largest and best known is the Frankfurt Book Fair, which is held each autumn, and where many publishers gather to show their wares rights managers sell and deal and the 'groupies' hang out. For children's books the annual Book Fair held in Bologna in March is important. The ABA (American Booksellers Association) is held in a different USA city each year. In the UK there is the London Book Fair. There are also the specialist book fairs which continue to grow in importance, such as the International Feminist Book Fair held every two years in a different country, the annual Socialist Book Fair, the Irish Book Fair held in London, SPG Annual Book Fairs held in September, National Convention of Poets and Small Press a moveable feast, Feminist Book Fortnight, yearly, usually June and the Anarchist Book Fair held in late October.

Distribution deals with processing orders as they arrive from the trade, packing and distributing books, invoicing and collecting money — 'pick, pack and dispatch' as it is called. In many publishing houses this work is contracted out to specialists or sometimes to larger publishing houses.

Once a book is printed, the distribution department (or a distributor on contract to the publisher) takes charge of warehousing stock and supplying books to trade customers (mostly wholesalers, bookshops and libraries). The distributor is also responsible for invoicing, order processing, stock, credit control and shipping.

The finance department prepares and analyses internal management information on the performance of the company as a whole. This includes annual budgets, profit and loss statements, cash-flow and balance sheets as well as payment of suppliers and the recording and payment of authors' royalties from book sales and rights.

The publisher: Traditionally the publisher was actually the editor or came from a printing background. Now more and more, the big multinational publishing companies seem to be headed by people with backgrounds in finance and marketing, which says a lot about how much the business has changed. The publisher has the central role in the press, co-ordinating all activities, sustaining and developing a definite editorial policy.

Some questions authors ask

There are several other aspects of the publishing business which would be useful for an author to know about. What is an ISBN, for instance? Why do all books have ISBN numbers? How do publishers fix the price of a book (which often seems exorbitant to the author and to bear little or no relation to her royalties!)? What is the Net Book Agreement and how does it affect authors? I deal with such questions briefly in this section.

Why is the price of my book so high?
Why do I not earn more from the sale of my book?
Why are my royalties so low?
Authors, and readers, often wonder why books are expensive and where the money goes. An author sees the price of her book (say £5.00) and understandably asks, 'Why am I only getting .25p of the published (retail) price on copies sold? What has happened to the rest of the money?'

It seems very unfair at first sight, especially when some authors receive royalties as low as 2-3 per cent on the price of a book and other authors get no royalties at all after spending months, if not years, writing their book. Generally, authors' earnings from the sales of their book are very low. If authors were to be paid even a reasonable hourly rate for their labour most books would never get published or would cost so much to buy that no copies would be sold.

The way it works is that the royalty an author receives is set by the publisher on the basis of costs and what the publisher expects the book to earn for both the author and publisher. However, the publisher of course only passes on to the author a share of the money she receives from the bookseller via the public. The booksellers' cut is based on the price of the book and most booksellers would argue that they too do not get enough.

A large slice of the book's published price, approximately 50 per cent, is taken in discounts by the publisher's main customers, the wholesaler, who buys in bulk (say 200 plus) and sells on copies of the book to the retailer (the bookseller), who gets 33 per cent (plus) of the published price. The publisher then pays the printer for the cost of manufacturing the book (15 per cent - 21 per cent of the published price), pays royalties to authors, commission to the reps and distributors who are selling to the book trade, fees to illustrators, readers etc. From the remainder the publisher has to cover her own staff and running costs!

Let's look at a particular book in detail. Take a paperback which sells for £5.00 (retail price) on a print run of 3,000 copies:

	%	£
Published Price:	100	5.00
Less discount to book trade	40%	2.00
Less production costs		
(artwork, setting, printing)	21%	1.05
Less royalty to author	7.5%	0.375
Less marketing budget	8%	0.40
Less distributor	7.5%	0.375
Less publisher's overheads	13%	0.65
TOTALS	.97	4.85
Giving the publisher a potential profit of	3%	0.15p

The publisher's overheads include salaries, representation, shipping, postage, rent, rates and office administration, giving a profit which may not exceed 3 per cent. You see from this example that the maximum profit the publisher can make on this particular book is £420.00! Presuming that 2,800 copies are sold in a year it can take up to four months before the publisher is paid and over eighteen months before the press gets back its outlay on a book.

Obviously, this is not a recipe for instant wealth for either publisher or author. The turnover of the entire British publishing industry comes nowhere near that of a single firm such as ICI and those who work in the publishing business rarely earn high salaries.

The major costs involved in the manufacture and selling of a book are paid out well before the publisher sees any financial return. It can take up to three years from the time your contract is signed to your book arriving on the bookshop shelf. The publisher's profit, if and when it does arrive, is most often ploughed back into the company for future projects, many of which will not bear fruit for many years. The distributor and bookseller also have their overhead costs to meet as well as trying to make a profit.

Given this breakdown of costs you may well ask how the average publisher manages to stay in business. For the larger publishing houses and the multinationals it has to do with sheer volume, the number sold, as well as central buying and services. For smaller publishers careful cash-flow and management of money over a long period of time is vital for survival. The books that sell will often subsidise other books. Then there is the 'backlist' which is often referred to as the financial backbone of a publishing house. In practice, small, independent publishing houses survive by not looking for the same level of profits as the big multinationals. Believe it or not, many publishers are in the business for the sheer love and excitement of it.

I cannot understand my royalty statement
I only get one royalty statement a year
My publisher has deducted sums of money from my royalties
Some authors feel their royalty statement is not detailed enough with publishers giving a shorthand version of sales. It has been my experience that authors feel their royalty statement is too complex and detailed. It is important,

however, that authors know (a) how many copies of their book have sold (or been returned) since their last royalty statement together with total sales of book to date (b) where these books have been sold ie Home, Europe, USA, Australia etc (c) how these books have been sold via wholesale, retail, bookclubs and so on (d) information on subsidiary, extract rights sales, etc.

There is no reason why publishers cannot issue two royalty statements per annum. However any resistance to supplying more regular statements has more to do with the fact that publishers have to wait up to three months (wholesale) and more (if overseas) before they receive payment from their customers. Although books ordered by the trade are registered as sales in the accounts system, the reality and 'norm' is that they are being sold on a 'sale or return' (on loan) basis. This means that your first royalty statement may show that 500 copies of your book has been sold, royalties are paid to you on these sales at the end of the accounting period. In the meantime 200 of these books are returned for credit (which means that you have been overpaid royalties on 200 books which never sold). The problem of returns has become so acute that the principle of holding a reserve of 20% against returns is now standard practice. If the publisher or distributor forces payment for unsold books the customer will just return them and sales may be lost or the book could be remaindered. Other deductions on your royalty statement may relate to purchases of books you have made.

PAYMENTS FOR SUBSIDIARY RIGHTS SALES (LICENSED RIGHTS)
The contract lists further rights (*see Glossary and chapter 6 on Contracts and Royalites*) granted to the publisher (unless otherwise agreed) which it could license to other publishers, and the percentages (eg 50-80 per cent) payable to the author on the publisher's net receipts from such sales. These may include reprint paperback rights (licensed to a separate paperback firm). If the publisher is granted, for example, North American book club and translation rights, the publisher to which these rights could be licensed may print their own editions and pay royalties to the publisher to be

shared with the author. However, the publisher may print bulk quantities of the book to appear under the new publisher's imprint. Because the original publisher has to sell on at a very high discount the author's royalty in this case may be inclusive of the sum received (eg 10 per cent). There are many other rights such as series and extract rights; dramatisation rights on stage, film, television and radio; broadcast reading rights; quotation and anthology rights (eg audio-cassette) etc. All or some of these rights may be termed 'subsidiary rights'.

My editor made drastic editorial changes to my book
My proof corrections were not followed
A fine balance must be maintained between your aspirations as an author and the realities of the marketplace. Usually editors have a lot of experience of dealing with written material and will honestly suggest rewrites, if they are necessary. It is well known that British and Irish publishers are quite reserved in helping authors to improve their books. They make oral or written suggestions to the authors hoping that they will take editorial advice. Then, later, they provide the service of making minor alterations to Mss such as punctuation, spelling, and the occasional change in phrasing, before it goes to the printers. You can of course refuse to accept the changes but you must be prepared for the fact that the publisher may refuse to publish the book. American publishers go to the other extreme and practically rewrite books without consulting the author. Authors and editors must be aware that even the most constructive criticisms can be met with hurt and argument.

The title of my book was changed without my approval
I was not consulted about cover design
My illustrations were not included
I disagreed with the blurb for my book
More and more contracts now include a clause which gives the author the right of consultation in relation to the title, cover design and illustrations. If the publisher has any sense she will listen to your comments, especially if you express the opinion that the illustration or the description of your

book is wrong. Of course the author has a right to refuse to approve the change but then the publisher can refuse to publish the book. Publishers do insist on having the final word as they believe they know more about selling books but again I believe in the strength and wealth of compromise.

Why am I responsible for compiling the index?
My publisher wants to charge me for indexing the book
The responsibility for obtaining any extraneous materials including permissions (quotations etc) and index should be the author's and not the publisher's. After all it is the author's work and the author would not expect the publisher to undertake the research or obtain any reference books or carry out interviews necessary for the book. However, the publisher should help the author with, for example, drafting a letter requesting permissions, and the question of paying for permissions (usually from another publisher) should be discussed. An agreement should be arrived at in advance and a budget set and adhered to. With regard to indexing, I think that the author should help identify the words and phrases she wants indexed by highlighting them on the hard copy. The index will be compiled in alphabetical order with cross referencing. In fact the author is the best person to do this, as she knows her own book best. Indexing is a highly skilled profession and publishers and indexers demand high standards. However, with computerisation, indexing should no longer be a long, laborious and expensive job and most publishers should be able to give more help to their authors now.

The publisher lost my Ms/materials/illustrations
Publishers receive several hundred Mss each year. Most publishers have a system of recording all material received with the date and name of author. However, you should always ensure that you keep a copy. If you send unsolicited material to a publisher you are responsible for insuring it. If you don't enclose a SAE the publisher is under no obligation to return it. If a publisher has accepted your Ms and materials, and you have requested their return in writing,

the publisher should take responsibility for any loss or damage.

My book was badly produced, with poor paper and small print
Yes, this can happen and sometimes, if it is not the printer's fault, it is because of efforts to economise and keep the retail price of the book down. But, no publisher wants a book to be so unpleasing as to affect its sales. However, design and size of print is very much a question of taste, and publishers tend to have their own 'look' for each particular book.

Why was the publication of my book delayed?
The publishing process can take a long time, and unforeseen delays can occur. Perhaps you did not meet your deadline; editorial work has taken longer than anticipated; another book has come out on the same subject and the publisher wants to wait; there has been a strike with the printers, a shortage of paper or a delay in its delivery. Most publishers do not want to delay publication because delays cost money. Whatever the reason you should be able to ask your publisher and get a reasonable response.

My publisher has demanded an unrealistic delivery date
A book is usually linked to some event or has to tie in with internal structures, in which case you may have to meet a particular deadline. The author should have been informed of this at the outset. You should keep your editor informed of your progress and if you have a problem state it immediately by discussion you may be able to sort it out together. If you find it impossible to meet the deadline you may have to give up the idea of writing the book.

My book has not been advertised
My book has received no reviews
All my reviews are unfavourable
Most publishers will tell you that advertising in the national media is very expensive and that such advertising does not sell books unless you have millions to spend on promoting blockbusters like Jackie Collins or Maeve Binchy. Publishers

spend their advertising budgets on the trade magazines and on various promotion tools like dumpbins (display units), posters, catalogues, bookmarks and so on.

Only a minority of books receive reviews in large numbers. It is the literary editors who decide what to review. It is much easier to get a mention in a local paper or radio than in the national media unless your are a big name or the book is saying something that is in the news or will make news. The publisher has no control over what the reviewers say. However, if you feel you are being badly treated you are entitled to write to the newspaper and say so. Most publishers subscribe to a press clippings service; if the book is reviewed these are filed and used to promote the book in other ways. The publisher is under no obligation to send you reviews but I am sure most would if you asked them; some publishers, like ourselves, send them out to authors every so often.

My book is not in the shops
My previous book sold more copies
These are probably the most common complaints that publishers receive. Sometimes it is the publisher's and distributor's fault orders are lost, wrong books are supplied or other human errors occur. But don't always presume it is the publisher's fault. Sometimes they cannot supply a particular bookshop, where the account has not been paid; the book may have just sold out or the bookseller may not be aware that the stock is out. Publishers don't want their books lying in the warehouse. They want sales. But there is nothing that a publisher can do to compel a bookseller to stock any book. Again you could politely ask the bookseller where your book is and if they have re-ordered it. You could also let the publisher know that your book is not available in such and such a shop.

My publisher won't answer my letters or phone calls
If you are a potential author it can take up to three months, if not six, for an editorial department to process the numbers of Mss they receive. However, most attempt to respond within three months. You should at least get an

acknowledgement (if you send a SAE). If you have not had a response within three months you are entitled to write again seeking a response or requesting your Ms back. It is important that there is a close working relationship between author and publisher. Publishers have to deal with hundreds of authors with limited resources in terms of time and staff. However, if you genuinely feel that you are being neglected you should be able to say so and the matter should be dealt with amicably on both sides.

My book was rejected for personal/political reasons
If there is no contract or agreement a publisher is under no duty or obligation to publish. A book can of course be rejected where the content would pose a threat of libel, or because a similar book is out or on the way. Or the publisher may decide that the writing is simply not of a high enough standard. You can of course try another publisher.

I put an idea to my publisher who rejected it. Then they commissioned another author to write a book on the same subject
If this is true it is highly unethical, but I feel that most publishers would not do this. Publishers and editors are very active and are constantly scouting; they receive inspiration from many sources at different times. A publisher will have a 3-5 year publishing plan with various ideas listed. What can happen, and I have experienced it many times, is that ideas converge; 'great minds think alike'. Ideas are not protected by copyright.

My contract bears no resemblance to the Minimum Terms Agreement (MTA)
Only members of the Society of Authors or the Writers' Guild are entitled to the full benefits of the MTA (just like a trade union). However, you could seek their advice if you have problems with your contract. The MTA does not apply to highly illustrated, technical or reference books, to manuals or books involving three or more participants. However, your problem may not be with the terms so much as an inability to understand what certain clauses in the

contract mean. If you don't have an agent and are not a member of the Society of Authors or the Writers' Guild you could simply ask the publisher to explain everything in the contract or approach another author or a lawyer. Many publishers will argue that they cannot afford to implement all the clauses of the MTA. You may find that some of the publisher's clauses are more generous than some of the MTA terms (*see Appendix D*) and less so in others; it is also a question of your own personal and reasonable judgement.

My publisher wants to break my contract
In a publishing contract the author agrees to write the book and the publisher undertakes to publish it. Publishing requires a massive amount of capital, and cash-flow can be a constant problem. Many publishers survived the recession of the 1980s and 1990s by reducing their output of books, especially those which were questionable in terms of profit margins. Others houses were gobbled up by multinationals and the editorial direction changed. Redundancies in the editorial department can lose you your friend. If you feel that your publisher is breaking your contract check first that you have fulfilled your contractual obligations. For instance, the publisher may feel that the work is not the same as that agreed to, that it is too short, too long, needs extensive revision which you have refused to do or are incapable of doing. You may have failed to meet your delivery date which was linked to an event or schedule. Perhaps the material is libellous. Just be sure of your ground and your own assessment of the situation. You can of course resort to legal action but this may prove difficult if not impossible. If you do succeed your relationship will not be a happy one. You could settle by asking for the remainder of your advance. In any case whether the fault lies with you or your publisher, you should ask for the return of your material and you are free to approach another publisher.

My publisher refuses to reprint my book
Authors sometimes worry that the publishers will allow their book to fall out of print. In fact, this is highly unlikely if the book is still selling. It is the sales department which is

primarily responsible for calling for a reprint. This is a decision which is always taken with a great deal of care because all copies of the publishers edition may have left the warehouse, but the sales people have to be sure that they have also left the booksellers' shelves and more importantly that there are enough orders to justify a reprint.

I have been asked to revise and update my book with no offer of an advance
My book has been remaindered
My book was published only six months ago and the publisher has lost interest in it
Most contracts state that the author agrees to update the book if it is necessary. The publisher will argue that a revised edition will generate more sales for your book and that your payment will come in the form of royalties. Remaindering a book is painful for the author and the publisher. Everybody loses out except the growing number of remainder shops. The author should be informed and given a chance to purchase copies of her book before they are remaindered. A book should not be remaindered for at least a year if possible. However, the shelf life of a book is becoming shorter and shorter and some would say books will soon have a shelf life similar to magazines. In most cases the sales potential of a book will have been achieved within six months of its publication. Additional effort and promotion by the publisher will not increase sales unless there is an event which can be linked to it or a film is released which is based on the book.

What is an ISBN?
As soon as the contract is signed, the press will request an ISBN for the book. The International Standard Book Number (ISBN) is individual to each book. It identifies one title, or an edition of a title, from one specific publisher and is unique to each book. It is solely designed to aid machine ordering of books the same system is used in a supermarket for products like, say, sugar. The system was set up in Britain in 1968. There is no legal requirement to have an ISBN but it is useful as many bookshops, libraries, distributors and

wholesalers use computerised ordering systems and rely on an ISBN for purchasing.

Most publishing houses are given blocks of ISBNs for a small fee, which they then allocate, informing the agency of the title and number allocation. If you are 'Self Publishing' your book, you can apply for an ISBN, free of charge, by writing to: Standard Book Numbering Agency, 12 Dyott Street, London WC1 Tel: (071) 836 8911.

What is an ISSN?
The International Standard Serial Number is for magazines and periodicals and relates closely to the ISBN system. For more information contact: The ISDS National Centre, National Library of Ireland, Kildare Street, Dublin 2.

What does CIP (Catalogue in Publication Data) mean?
This is an important marketing and sales tool. CIP information appears on the preliminary pages (technical page) in a book. The CIP system was set up in 1978 to provide detailed advance bibliographic information on forthcoming books. It is run by the British Library. The list of books which have been allocated CIPs are published in trade directories used by librarians and booksellers for their ordering, and in the 'Weekly List' of the British National Bibliography. Again, the publisher applies for CIP by filling in supplied forms which will be returned to the press. The CIP includes the ISBN. The CIP obtained from the British Library is for books published in Britain and Ireland. Books published in the USA have their own CIP data supplied by the Library of Congress.

What is Retail Price Maintenance (RPM) or NBA (Net Book Agreement)?
A Net Book is a book with a fixed price set in advance by the publisher. The book is then sold at the same price everywhere and prices are not increased when demand is high. However, in the summer of 1992 the European Community (EC) ruled against a Resale Price Maintenance (RPM) system operating in one country (ie Britain) and

applying in any other country of the Community (ie Ireland). The EC has no objection whatever to the various RPM systems which apply in ten of the twelve member states but it doesn't permit their transnational application.

Many people including authors, publishers, librarians, booksellers and readers believe it to be essential that the stability of a fixed retail price on books is maintained. They believe that innovation, experimentation, and risk-taking are the lifeblood of books and that if quality, information, education and entertainment is to flourish it is essential that the RPM be retained. Without the RPM the reading public will suffer because new, young and not so well-known authors will get squeezed out.

There are plenty of examples of the damage resulting from the policy of no retail price maintenance of books. In France up to 1981 the seller was free to decide the retail price. This resulted in rampant price wars, with the closure of bookshops and a reduction in the availability of less popular titles. In 1981 the French government stepped in and imposed RPM on books by law. A similar statutory arrangement also applies in Spain. In the USA, where there is no price control, there are fewer bookstores per head of the population, as well as inferior choice and service. When Australia abolished the NBA in 1971 the price of books increased resulting in a reduction in the quality and variety of books as well as staff redundancies. Bookshops in Ireland and Britain will now be faced with increasing their stock of 'bestsellers' and reducing the slower selling academic, alternative and serious titles. The large publishers, bookshops and chains will prosper but some of the smaller independent shops and publishers may go out of business.

3 Becoming an Author

Introduction

Writers start as readers. Before you begin to write you must have some idea of what you want to write about. Everybody has a bright 'idea' at some stage and it is presumed that writers have them more easily than other people. This may or may not be so; the point for you, as a potential 'author', is to work out how to turn your idea into a book that will interest people enough to want to buy it. But before you get to your reader you must know what publishers are looking for – books that will sell and make money, you may be tempted to say, cynically. In fairness, authors want their books to be read and the vast majority want to make at least some money in the process.

Most publishers do not know exactly what they are looking for but they certainly know it when they find it. They study the market, and market trends, very closely and are acutely aware of what their competitors are doing. Publishers build their lists at least partly on this basis, but then there is the indefinable and essential 'nose' factor, without which no publishing house will flourish. This is the ability to sniff out a good idea and see the possibility hidden away there.

There are of course essential criteria which most publishers and editors look for when selecting a Ms or commissioning something, whether it is a blockbuster or a book about the effects of soap on your toes. The points below are all worth thinking about before you launch yourself and your Ms on the path to publication.

1. The overall *presentation of the submitted Ms or outline* can tell the editor a lot about the author and her attitude and commitment. Most publishers will refuse to even consider handwritten Mss other than in the most exceptional circumstances. But a poorly presented, untidy Ms can also be interpreted as arrogance. Be aware of the importance of first impressions! While good professional presentation

alone is no guarantee of acceptance it will get you a sympathetic reading. So give your work what it deserves - your best, and possibly, only chance.

2. When your Ms is being read, spelling, accuracy and punctuation will all be noticed as well as the correct use of words. The style and phrasing of your sentences, the shape and construction of paragraphs and chapters as well as your ability to communicate with clarity are crucial. Avoid waffle, ie don't present your subject like an overdressed bishop and don't show off. Easy or lazy writing can make for hard reading and a good editor can spot this a mile off. Take a hard look at your proposal or Ms and ask yourself if you really have something to say to the reader and if you are managing to say it clearly. This applies especially to non-fiction.

3. It is vital for your opening to appeal to the reader immediately – to 'grab' her attention.

4. If you are writing a novel, ask yourself if the characters are credible, if there is a sense of time and place. Will the readers really believe what they are being told?

5. Publishers think in terms of thousands of words, and so should you. An average novel is around 200 pages (70,000 - 80,000 words) and a blockbuster usually contains 200,000 plus words. Study the size and style of your competition in terms of illustrations, chapter arrangement, index, glossary, etc.

6. For non-fiction ask yourself if you convey a sense of authority and knowledge of your subject.

Books that don't sell (or **What not to write**)
There are of course bad books which sell well and good books which flop for no obvious reason; maybe it's the 'hype', or being in the wrong place at the wrong time. However, there are certain kinds of books that most publishers will approach only very gingerly, and others that they will not touch at all. There is also no doubt that public taste is fickle and sometimes refuses to follow 'market trends'.

Publishers are rarely interested in *autobiographies* unless the person is famous, or has an extended family of 1,500 avid readers. *Biographies* of obscure people are also 'no no's'. Publishing houses with general lists will rarely consider *poetry* or *short stories*. Although interest in poetry has increased in recent years, sales are still very low. The problem with short stories is that although many people will swear they love them, collections just don't sell. The best place for short stories is in the occasional anthology and even then there is a limited market. Novels about failure or with highly contrived plots are out, as are expensive coffee-table books (odd size, highly illustrated, with pop-out gimmicks) except to packagers. Publishers will not touch potentially libellous books, because they cannot afford to - authors just don't have the resources to reimburse the publisher and distributor in the event of a court case.

What you should concentrate on
A subject that you know. This is old advice, but absolutely sound. Concentrate on what you know best or what you can research most thoroughly. Don't set yourself up as an 'overnight expert' — it won't fool a sharp-eyed editor for an instant. Knowledge and expertise alone are no guarantee of success, of course. You must be interested in your subject or, at the very least, be able to communicate a sense of involvement and enthusiasm — even passion. Though you may be a specialist in pensions, for example, there is no point in writing a book about this fascinating subject if the thought of writing about pensions bores you rigid and you are passionately interested in coins or the sex life of clock watchers outside office hours. If the subject bores you, then it will bore your readers.

Subjects that interest other people, not just your family who want you to write it out of your system or their hair but an idea that you have tried out on impartial potential readers. Is there a big enough market for the book? Will the publisher be able to identify more than 1,500 people who will buy it?

An original idea. Often what publishers mean by this is that it's a well tried idea, proven to be popular but given a new angle or approach by a new author. The publisher is looking for originality combined with a safe bet. Many, many books have been published on computers, dieting, deep-freezers, but few have been bestsellers.

Whatever you write, **knowing your audience** (market) is key. Authors tend to be voracious readers. You can't write a book that people will want to read unless you know which books people *do* read.

A good working title will help you focus on the theme. It is too easy to get side tracked and go rambling off down side streets.

Join a writing group. If you want to start writing seriously or have been writing for some time but have no idea whether what you're doing is interesting to other people, get involved in a writing group. You can fly your ideas past group members, get feed-back from their response to your work and learn a great deal about technique and style from listening to others and discussing joint problems.

Because You Want to Write: A Guide to women and writing, by Pearlie McNeil is aimed at the new writer, and those wishing to develop their writing skills. It is packed with ideas, exercises and strategies to help with the nuts and bolts of writing - language, imagery, character, plot, narrative, dialogue and humour. *The Attic Guidebook and Diary* also contains a list of local groups. You can also contact your local library, newspaper, VEC, WEA, *Guide To Evening Courses* and so on.

The essential tools of your trade
Of course an idea, talent, encouragement, faith in yourself, determination, patience and some luck are essential for your writing success. Although books have been written under the most extraordinary and appalling conditions, the basic physical aids do help:

• Table and chair
• Paper
• Pen and pencil

- Typewriter or preferably a word-processor (or make friends with somebody who has one).
- Notebooks (for ideas, logging information, recording expenses, and work tasks)
- Files for cuttings and correspondence
- Card index file (for facts and figures or information on characters, places and events)
- Reference Books: Directories, maps, dictionary, Thesaurus and a copy of every available publication on your subject to add to your knowledge, to check your approach and to get your facts right (especially for biography and non-fiction), (see **Reading List**).
- If you have a telephone, get an answering machine to keep distraction at bay.
- A room of your own, as Virginia Woolf put it, or time to spend in one — even if it's at 5.00 in the morning or at midnight.

Preparing your proposal

One of the harshest realities of a writer's life is that most of the books which get published are commissioned. This is especially true of the big multinational and general publishing houses. It's also a fact that first-time authors, who do not yet have a 'track record', obviously have most difficulty in getting their Ms read and accepted. It's not at all unusual for authors to approach a number of different publishers before having their Ms accepted. There are endless stories of bestselling or highly acclaimed authors (the two don't necessarily go together!) who have approached seven, ten or even fifteen publishing houses before getting an acceptance.

You may be tempted to send off your entire Ms to the publishing house you have chosen, on the basis that they will undoubtedly want to read it all immediately. This is not actually very sensible as publishers are inundated with unsolicited Mss and are busy, deadline orientated people. It is far better to send in an outline of your Ms with one or two short extracts which will entice the editor or Ms reader. This is what is known as a *proposal*.

You should send a preliminary letter to the editor of the

press (it's not necessary to know her name), with an outline of the proposed book for non-fiction, and a synopsis for fiction or else a brief sample. Enclose a SAE. The publisher is not responsible for any loss or damage to your work so take great care before you make your decision to submit your proposal and always keep a copy for yourself. You may have to wait some time for a response but if you have heard nothing after three months, you should write to the publisher asking if they wish to follow-up with you or if they are considering a rejection. In reality your Ms will have to wait in the queue to be assessed by one or two publishers' readers.

It is unwise to send your full Ms to a publishing house before being asked to, but if you decide to go ahead anyway, please remember to enclose sufficient stamps or a postal/money order for packing and return of your Ms. The publisher is under no obligation whatsoever to either acknowledge receipt of or to return your Ms. Publishers can receive thousands of requests each year and they do not have the time or resources to run an information bureau.

Submitting your proposal

It's obvious that the more targeted and professional your approach, the higher your chances of having your idea seriously considered. Your proposal should be typed/word processed and contain as a minimum the following information, on not more than six pages:

1. The covering letter to the Editor, on one page, with a summary, in one paragraph, of about 200 - 300 words outlining the scope and content of your book and showing the originality of your approach.
2. A contents list with a brief description of each chapter, even if the book is not finished.
3. A realistic assessment of: potential readers (ie children, stamp collectors), and markets (local, national and or international).
4. Is there a similar book on the market? If so, say what the competing books are, when they were published, by whom and at what price. How does yours compare?

5. A short paragraph describing what stage you are at, ie how many chapters you have written, how many more need to be completed, how long (approx) the final text will be. Say whether your book requires any illustrations such as maps, diagrams, tables or photographs.

6. Are you working on a typewriter or computer? What way will the Ms be presented, ie typed with two hard copies or on a disc with one print out of the final edition (hardcopy). If relevant, give the make of computer (ie Apple, Amstrad or PC) and the name of software you are using (ie Wordstar, Wordperfect, Word etc. *(see Appendix G* on Keying in your text on a word-processor)

7. Give a brief description of yourself (biography) including your relevant experience and/or qualifications. Have you been published before?

8. Is there a possibility of your being able to get sponsorship for the book through a relevant organisation, ie a book on housing might be part funded by an organisation involved with this issue.

9. Please be courteous and tell the editor if you have sent your idea/Ms to other publishers for consideration.

10. Also state if you have an agent or intend hiring an agent at this initial contact stage.

11. Finally, think in a business-like way.

Submitting your manuscript

As I've said, it is very unwise to send your Ms without being asked to do so. Generally speaking, you should only send your full Ms to a publisher on request. You will usually send a developed proposal first, as just outlined. When you do submit your Ms, there are several very important points to bear in mind.

General presentation

Before finalising the text of your Ms ask the publisher to send you a copy of their *house style* and *notes on preparing your Ms on Disc*, if they have them. If your publisher has a particular house style a lot of time, energy and expense will be saved if you follow their preferred form on layout, punctuation and so on. It stands to reason that the better presented your Ms, the smoother its passage will be through editorial and production.

Check-list before sending Ms to publisher

• Make sure that all your references (quotations and bibliographical details) give the publisher's full name with the year of publication; that statistics, dates of events and spellings are correct; that all abbreviations are explained and that all references, abbreviations and glossary are in alphabetical order. If you want to query something, make a note in the margin to the copy-editor.

• Check that notes relate correctly to text and that cross-references to sections, figures and so on still apply after revision. Check that the numbering systems used for headings, figures, notes, maps, diagrams and plates are in order and that none are missing or repeated. If a page cross reference is essential, type 'p.000' in text (the page number will be filled in later).

• Check through the Ms for phrases which would make the book date too quickly, for example, 'this year' 2001 (or which suggest a restricted readership for example 'in this country'). Just put the exact date and the name of the country. You can widen the market for your book by making sure that special terms are clearly explained.

• Keep a copy of all material and correspondence sent to a publisher with a note of telephone conversations and appointments made.

• Confirm any oral arrangements in writing.

• Always enclose SAE for return of your MS.

• If you have not heard from the publisher after three months make gentle enquiries by letter or telephone.

• If and when your Ms is finally accepted, make sure you see your contract, take time to go through it, take advice, be sure you are satisfied about payments and terms, ie how much, when you will get it. Ask the publisher what she expects the retail price of the book to be and roughly how many books they expect to sell (a) wholesale and (b) retail, Your royalty percentage is dependent on this. *(see Chapter 6)*

Typewriter or word-processor?

The short answer is that in any stand-off between a word-processor and a typewriter, the word-processor wins every time. Word-processing can make your job as an author so much easier, especially when you are asked to make changes. Some authors do prefer to, literally, write their 'manuscript', to allow the creative process flow. One way or another, your Ms must be presented in an ultra-clean, legible copy to your publisher. Nowadays, most publishers prefer, and some expect, to receive word-processed Mss. A Ms received on disc is much easier and quicker to process than a typescript, which will have to be laboriously keyed in for a second time.

Keying in your text on a typewriter

If you are using a typewriter, there are a few points you need to take special note of:

- Give the chapter title on top of each page.
- Indent the first line of each new paragraph.
- For a typescript, if you want to insert something or suggest an alternative, it must be typed on a separate A5 page and numbered in relation to the relevant page. For example, if the insertion is for page 12, mark the insertion page 12a and mark clearly on page 12 where text is to be inserted.
- Indicate breaks in your text with an asterisk (*).
- Number each heading and subheading (especially in non-fiction Mss) and grade them in order of importance (see section on House Style).

Keying in your text on a word-processor

Converting and setting text from an author's disc helps the publisher to minimise typographical errors as the text does not have to be re-keyed in. Reproduction from disc means the author has to be very careful, but it does give you more control over your final work. Text from disc also helps control the time and cost of producing the book. When submitting discs, you must *always* submit a hardcopy (printout) of your text. Do remember to keep a back-up copy for yourself of all discs you send to the publisher, for reference and safe keeping as well as insurance against loss. *(see Appendix G* Keying your in text on a word-processor)

4 Making Money from Writing

Making a living

Without doubt the greatest reward of writing for most authors will be the reward of writing for its own sake. There is also great satisfaction in the feelings of sheer pleasure and accomplishment that comes from expressing yourself creatively and reading your completed work, even if it is never published. Of course, if your work is published there is the added sense of achievement and excitement that comes with seeing your writing in print and your name on the cover of a book. Finally there may be the bonus of earnings, although this is far more rare than most people think.

Despite what you read and hear about vast fortunes being made by certain bestselling authors, these success stories are few and far between. Writing is a tough and often lonely profession, requiring great stamina and skill. If you think about the fact that over 70,000 new books are being published in Britain and Ireland each year (representing less than one per cent of what is being accepted by publishers for publication) your chances of appearing in print are quite slim. But let's hope that after reading and following the advice in this book you may become one of the lucky 70,000 and have the good fortune to find yourself with an advance of either £100, £250 or £500. This is scarcely riches and, indeed, few authors are obliged to become tax exiles.

Most authors' earnings are small and uncertain and rarely exceed the advance received before the book hits the shelves. So you can see that unless you can either multiply those earnings by writing an impossibly high number of books or supplement your income with grants, awards, bursaries, prizes or by writing freelance articles, giving talks and interviews, your first step will be to try and avoid falling into the debt trap. To do this you need to take a realistic view of your potential earnings and costs. The cost of writing can be quite high and the vast majority of writers never calculate it! Even if you do eventually become a household name, you will find that it can take some time before cheques start coming on a regular basis. Most of your earnings can be wiped out by those legitimate expenses incurred in purchasing the tools of your trade in order to set yourself up as a writer.

You must learn to balance your income against your expenditure. And remember, you are also supposed to declare all income to the Revenue, however small. You may well be storing up trouble for yourself if you don't.

Taxation

Once you get paid for writing, whether you are supplementing your income by writing books, articles, short stories or poems, other than in the course of your paid employment (full-time, part-time, or freelance), the Revenue people see you, even if you don't, as embarking on a business venture and you are considered to be self-employed. So you will be taxed on your royalties. Sales of copyright are also taxable they are treated as income and not as capital receipts. Sums paid on account of, or in advance of, royalties are also taxable as income in the year of receipt. Copyright royalties are generally paid without deduction of income tax. If royalties are paid to a person who normally lives abroad, tax will be deducted at source unless arrangements are made with the Revenue for payments to be made gross.

However, it may be possible that your expenses for freelance writing, or indeed writing a book, exceed your writing income and that you may be able to offset or reclaim tax on surplus expenses on other income. The Revenue people have been known to try and treat casual writing as a hobby so that losses incurred cannot be used to reclaim tax even though they will treat income receivable as taxable.

Taxation is not only about income it is also about your expenses and costs. Tax should only be paid on income that exceeds your tax allowance limit. Your tax limit is determined by the amount of legitimate expenses you can claim. You can only claim these expenses if you keep a copy of all bills for purchases, receipts of payments and have your books in order, otherwise you may end up paying unnecessary taxation.

You should first of all set yourself an annual income target and then work on the details of how to reach this. It is also worth your while seeking financial advice, especially on tax matters. Whether you decide to hire an accountant or not is up to you but remember that writing is a business and one way or the other you should set up a tight financial control system and keep a very close eye on everything that you purchase or that you can attribute as a cost in the excercise of your profession. It may be worth your while to receive some payments as reimbursement for expenses.

It is also very important not to confuse your income and expenditure if you have two jobs or two sources of income as there may be difficulty in claiming 'duality of purpose' expenses, ie the grey area of expenditure which reflects private and business use. Great tact and care should be taken when dealing with the Revenue in negotiating travelling expenses, telephone, food, clothing, for example. If provoked they may well allow you nothing. The clothing must be of a particular type and not just used in the interest of public decency or for everyday use. The same with food — is it being used to sustain life or in order to work? There is no tax relief for the cost of entertainment and before you claim travelling expenses you should first get professional advice.

The following expenditure is usually allowed if you can show invoice and payment records:
1. Cost of writing, typing, typesetting, proofing, secretarial and research expenses
2. Normal business expenditure such as pens, tippex, ribbons, postage and other stationery expenses
3. Telephone (including rental), answering machines, fax, photocopier. (*see Chapter 10. Capital allowances*)
4. Agent's fees, accountancy charges
5. Subscriptions, reference books, specialist periodicals and magazines, daily newspapers
6. Visits to theatres, cinemas etc for your research purposes only, and not your partner or guest!
7. If you work from home, a reasonable proportion of the

rent, light and heating bills, cleaning, maintenance and insurance. Be careful not to allocate a specific workroom exclusively for business purposes; this may result in partial forfeiture of Capital Gains Tax exemption on the house as the only main residence. Claim a deduction on the basis that most or all of the rooms in the house are used at one time or another for business purposes.

8. Travel and hotel expenses if you can prove that it was not a holiday.

9. If you have a separate business bank account and you have overdraft interest this will be an allowable expense.

10. Capital allowances can be claimed for a television, car, video recorder or tape recorder, typewriter, computer and other business machinery, office furniture as well as the cost of maintenance and repair of same which is used for business purposes. But remember that where expenditure of a capital nature is incurred, it cannot be deducted from income as an expense (as is 3 above). Again you need careful advice and planning here because plant and machinery qualify for a 25 per cent allowance in the year of purchase and 25 per cent of the reducing balance in subsequent years, but there can be additional problems and disadvantages if the equipment is leased.

11. If you are self-employed and pay annual premiums under an approved personal pension policy, you are entitled to tax relief.

Authors' tax exemption — Ireland

You should get yourself a set of guidelines from the Revenue Commissioners explaining the relevant sections of the 1969 Finance Act which give details on earnings from original and creative works, which are exempt from income tax.

Authors' earnings from original and creative works are exempt from income tax under the 1969 Finance Act. To qualify for relief the author must be resident in the state, for income tax purposes, and not resident elsewhere.

An individual seeking relief must apply to the Revenue and fill in either: (a) Artists 1 Form, stating that she or he has produced a work or works generally recognised as having cultural or artistic merit or alternatively, (b) Artists 2 Form, submitting a particular work of hers or his which has been published, produced or sold and requesting a determination that such work has cultural or artistic merit.

'Work' means an original and creative work in any of the following categories:
(i) a book or other writing, (ii) a play, (iii) a musical composition, (iv) a painting or other like picture, (v) a sculpture; which may have been written, composed or executed either solely by the person seeking the determination or jointly with another individual.

The forms may be obtained and returned to the Office of the Revenue Commissioners, Room 2, Cross Block, Dublin Castle. The Revenue Commissioners then submit the work to an authority (usually the Arts Council) for a judgement as to whether the work fulfils the terms of the Act. Exemption is much harder to get than it used to be. If you intend earning your living from creative writing you should investigate this possibility because you could earn £50,000 and pay no tax. This is one of the reasons why so many international writers have taken up residency in Ireland. However, the work should be what is considered 'artistic' (fiction, poetry and drama); works of fact (non-fiction) do not qualify, even if they are bestsellers.

Grants

Grants are available from The Arts Council in Ireland which is the statutory body appointed to promote and assist the Arts in Ireland mainly by giving advice and financial assistance. Grants are divided into two categories, those which are to be treated as chargeable to tax and those which are not. Those that are, include grants to assist with a specific project or projects (such as the writing of a book). Literary prizes are not generally considered to be part of the author's professional income and may not be chargeable to tax. But be careful and seek professional advice.

The Council defines Irish literature as 'all of the imaginative writing produced on the island of Ireland, whether it be from northern Ireland or the Republic, or by Irish writers abroad, whether it be in the Irish language or

the English language.' The Arts Council assists literature under four main headings:
1. The Writer; 2. Literary Organisations; 3. Publishers; 4. Magazines.

VAT

Although there is no VAT on books in Ireland or Britain at present VAT can be payable on royalties and advances, agency and accountancy fees, as well as on all those purchases of stationery and equipment you make in the course of your business. As soon as you expect your income to exceed (£15,000 in Ireland and £35,000 in Britain) you must register for VAT. Ironically, you can claim this back but only if you are registered, and authors whose income is less than the limit cannot — the less well off pay more. However, you might find that the amount of paperwork to be completed far outweighs the benefits.

Social security contributions

Every individual who works either as an employee or as a self-employed person is liable to pay social security contributions when income exceeds £2,500pa. You should check not only the rates but any benefits.

Public Lending Rights (PLR)

Although the PLR applies in relatively few countries and does not apply in Ireland it is an interesting model for possible expansion. Brigid Brophy and Maureen Duffy spearheaded an intensive lobbying campaign over several years resulting in the passing of the British Public Lending Right Act of 1979. The women, with the backing of the Society of Authors, the Writer's Guild and other interested parties succeeded in establishing the right that authors, who are registered with the PLR, receive a payment every time their book is borrowed through the public library system. The PLR only came into operation in February 1984. As these payments belong exclusively to you, the author, the onus is entirely on you, and not on your publisher or agent, to apply for registration to the PLR office. If you think you are eligible you should write for a form to: Public Lending Right, Bayheath House, Prince Regent Street, Stockton-on-Tees, Cleveland TS18 1DF.

You are eligible:
• If you are an author (ie writer, illustrator, translator and some editors/compilers) and your name appears on the title page of a book – it does not matter if you have sold copyright.
• If you are a British citizen or a citizen of an EC country and your main home is in the UK or Germany (reciprocal arrangement). The author must be alive at the time of registration.
• If your book is borrowed, or lent out through British public library system under the PLR.
• If your book is published and registered. It does not matter when your book was published or if it is out of print. If it is in the library and can be borrowed it can earn you royalties under the PLR.

How the PLR works
The borrowings of registered books, from a sample of thirty public libraries, in various parts of the country, are recorded for a period of twelve months and an average is then taken for the country as a whole. Academic, private or commercial libraries are not included in the scheme, nor are the reference sections of public libraries. It is interesting to note that the PLR depends on the ISBN to identify books and to correlate loans, unfortunately not all publishers use bar codes or print the ISBN number on the back cover.

Payment is made once a year (February) from a public fund of just under £5 million, after administration costs have been deducted. There are limits to the payments authors receive. No payment is made if the author's earnings are less than £1 per year and no payment can exceed £6,000 in any one year.

At last count nearly 183,000 books were registered for PLR – or approximately 20,200 authors (including 610 German authors). Forty per cent of all library borrowings (568 million loans) qualified for the PLR. The rest (60 per cent) were ineligible for various reasons, eg books written by dead or foreign authors or books not registered under the PLR. Eighty-one of the most popular authors earned £6,000 under the PLR, another 226 authors received between £2,500 and £5,999, 501 between £1,000 and £2,499, 3,637 between £100 and £999 and 11,653 authors received payments between £1 and £99. Another 3,339 registered authors received nothing. The top 82 earning authors (50/50 male/female), Archer, Binchy, James, Taylor Bradford, Cartland, Christie, Collins, Cooper, Cookson, Dahl, Francis, Blyton, King, Rendell, Robins, Steel, Smith etc, represent 12.3 per cent or nearly 70,101,000 loans.

5 Literary Agents

If you are writing fiction or general non-fiction you are much more likely to require the services of a Literary Agent, than if you are the author of academic or school books. However, a good agent is actually more difficult to find than a publisher! In fact, the top agents tend to chase authors rather than the other way round. An important part of an agent's energy goes into seeking out and promoting new writers and supporting them. Still, not every agent can be all-knowing, so if you are very keen on being represented, it's worth sending samples of your work 'on spec' to several agents or agencies who specialise in your kind of writing.

What Literary Agents Do

• Sell your work by sending 'professional' submissions, at their own expense, to appropriate publishers on your behalf
• Use their experience and knowledge of the market — who is buying, looking for or specialising in what, where and when — and matching your needs with theirs, as well as keeping you in contact with the complex world of publishing. This can be especially useful if you are not living close to the hub of the publishing world — or if you are living abroad.
• Negotiate advance payments, royalty percentages, contract terms and explain details of these to you as well as collecting money and checking royalty statements for any errors
• Sell different rights to your work to different publishers and markets, for example, paperback, hardback, translation and film rights
• Act as a buffer and filter between you and a publisher, especially during any disputes over contracts, for example
• Some Agents offer editorial advice and can even play a role in shaping and developing your writing career. But remember, Agents, like Publishers are not charities and you really should join a writing group if you require detailed advice on how to improve your writing.

• If your income comes from a mixture of writing books and/or journalism, radio, film, an agent is more essential for you. The larger agencies employ specialist staff for the different media.

Disadvantages

• Agents' charges range between 10 - 25 per cent + VAT, depending on rights sold. Depending on your earnings, this may seem rather high – or a small price to pay for saving you a good deal of time and trouble.

• Authors tend to express far more dissatisfaction with their agents, both past and present, than with their publisher. Occasionally, agents and editors have been known to have personality clashes. Publishers find some Agents off-putting and difficult to deal with. Most maintain a respectful distance and prefer to receive all submissions direct from an agent as they know that a submission received via an agent usually has some merit.

• Some agents have blind spots especially with smaller, and specialist publishing houses. It has been our experience in Attic Press that many UK-based agents never approach Irish publishing houses – they just don't see them. You can of course tell your agent to approach specific publishers on your behalf.

• Agents prefer to handle authors whose books can be placed easily and will sell in high quantities. If your book has already suffered several rejections few agents are likely to be interested in you.

If you plan or hope to earn a substantial part of your income from writing then an agent can be very useful. However, if you expect your earnings to average around £1,500 a year you will find it difficult to persuade an agent to take you on. You would need to be earning £5,000 a year to yield a mere £500 return for your agent, out of which she will have to pay wages, overheads and so on. So be realistic. Just as publishers exist from the money they make from their efforts on your behalf and in the hope that they will get a return on their investment, so do literary agents make their living from the commission they earn from selling your work.

Finding an agent

How you go about finding an agent, and the approach you take, is much the same as for finding a publisher. Some Agencies are general and some specialist. Some handle mostly fiction, others non-fiction. Some authors prefer large agencies while others feel, like the publishing house, that the small company may give more attention to detail and offer a more personalised service which is not totally oriented towards the big 'stars'.

Before making your approach you should first consult the *Writers' and Artists' Yearbook* and the *Writer's Handbook* to study the different types of agents and possibly seek advice from The Society of Authors (UK) or Irish Writers' Union. Your chances of finding a suitable agent increase of course if you can get a personal introduction. However you make your approach you must sell yourself and come across as efficient and businesslike. The largest agencies receive around 1,000 submissions every year and may take on as few as four or five new authors. So the more professional your approach in the first instance the better your chances of being read. You may find it easier to start with the smaller agencies and don't despair — many successful authors begin by submitting their work directly to a publisher.

Introductory letter

Initially, you write a short introductory letter to establish whether the Agent is interested in you as a potential client. State the stage your book is at and describe it and yourself accurately and concisely in three paragraphs.

Yourself: List your previous work and give any promotable features, for example, if you are writing a cookery book and you have won some award, give your qualifications - if these are detailed or complicated attach a well laid-out Curriculum Vitae (CV).

For a work of Fiction: Describe the book in two paragraphs. Outline the plot first succinctly, then state the genre, the period (if it's historical fiction), who you think is likely to be interested in it and give the approximate length.

For a work of Non-Fiction: State the subject area, the type of book you envisage, length, any illustrations and why you think there is a market for it.

You should always inform an agent if you have approached a publisher, at the time of submitting your work, and likewise let a publisher know if you have or intend getting an agent. I have known authors who have made direct contact with our Press and, as soon as we have shown an interest, they then introduced their agent – this is irritating and time wasting and not particularly fair dealing, so do avoid it as it only leads to bad feelings.

You can ask for the agent's terms and do remember to enclose a SAE. Don't send a full synopsis or specimen chapters until you are asked.

A few words of caution: as in your dealings with a publisher, be wise and do not expect too much too soon. For example, 'phoning your agent every two weeks to ask if your Ms has been accepted is likely to get on their nerves and will do nothing to make you a favourite client. It takes some months to place work with a publisher, so be patient. Never phone an agent, or publisher, on Friday afternoon or Monday morning!

Agents, publishers and editors do not exist to teach people how to write and you should not expect them to comment at length on work they consider unsuitable although sometimes they may do so. Some agencies are prepared to give an author a report and advice on their Ms and will make an appropriate charge for this (publishers don't!). Most agents will suggest revisions by the author, if the Ms is worthwhile and in certain cases the agency may recommend a freelance editor to work with you on the revisions. In a few cases the agent herself will undertake the revisions. Some agents also charge a reading fee for considering a first work. The fee should be returned to you if your book is eventually accepted for publication.

6 Contracts and Royalties

Contracts

Your contract is a key document and it is vital for you to be very clear about what you are being offered and what you are selling to the publisher. If you have an agent, she will negotiate your contract directly with the publisher, although it makes sense for you to indicate your preferences to your agent. If you are negotiating the contract yourself I hope this chapter will help you through the labyrinth of rights, percentages and legal conditions.

A contract is an agreement, legally binding, between author and publisher. An agreement is needed to identify, as clearly as possible, the areas of responsibility of both parties. It must be honoured in both letter and spirit by the publisher and the author.

The purpose of the agreement is to minimise financial risk, maximise control of production, distribution and promotion for the publisher while the author should have the security of knowing that the book will be published with a proper payment plan for royalties. An agreement should comply, as far as possible, with the Code of Practice drawn up by the Publishers Association (*see Appendix E*) and with the Minimum Terms of Agreement (MTA) drawn up by the Society of Authors and Writers' Guild (*see Appendix D*).

The agreement may appear daunting at first sight but it defines in detail the formal relationship between the author and publisher. It should be clear, unambiguous and comprehensive. Like all contracts, the publisher/author contract should be taken seriously and studied with care as the rights and liabilities between the author and publisher endure long after the point of publication.

One overall effect of a good publishing contract should be to place rights in the hands of those best able to exploit them in the interests both of the widest availability of the book and also in terms of income to the author and to those who work for the author, eg publisher or literary agent. The author must be able to maximise earnings, while publishers must be able to protect their investment in an author's work from unreasonable competition.

Because most authors are unable to market the rights on their work worldwide they mainly allow publishers to do so on their behalf. But an author may employ a literary agent, on commission, who may limit the rights granted to a publisher, and their territorial extent, and sell the rights retained on behalf of the author to other publishing houses at home and abroad. For instance, the publisher's licence may apply to the English language only, and the territory (the countries covered) in which it has the exclusive right to publish.

Raising the contract

When a decision is taken in-house to go ahead with publication, the publisher makes the author an offer, usually stating the amount of the advance and basic royalties. Many publishers have a standard contract as far as conditions are concerned with only the specifics of rights and percentages changing from contract to contract. But this is by no means always the case.

One of the main problems for an author is that publishers' contracts vary from house to house and from book to book within each house. Why should a publisher offer the same terms to a first-time author, as to an author with a proven track record? This is neither surprising nor evidence of sharp practice. Every book, author and publisher is different. There are good ones and bad ones and the vast majority of them are just average.

When the contract is raised a draft copy is sent to the author for signature. Any changes are marked and initialled on the first and then on a second copy. Both copies are signed, one kept by the author and the second filed by the publisher. The publisher's copy may be referred to many times, for example, when subsidiary rights are being considered and sold, preparing royalty statements and so on. You should never be rushed into signing your contract. Your publisher should give you or your agent reasonable time to study the document and should also explain any terms that are unclear and give reasons, if asked, for the inclusion of particular clauses.

Both authors and publishers may have real grievances from time to time. There are rogues, as in any profession, but such publishers tend not to survive. When authors have a genuine grievance there are procedures such as the arbitration clause in the contract which they are fully entitled to use if they believe they are being hard done by. Equally, there are authors who try to squeeze their publishers too hard, forgetting that publishing is a high risk business with very low profit margins. Overall, though, it is not in a publisher's interest to take an author for a ride any more than it is in the author's interest to push the publisher so hard that they end up withdrawing the offer.

Non contract issues

Even the best consultation clause in a contract cannot force a publisher to produce the type of book they do not wish or intend to produce. You are much more likely to be satisfied with your publisher's performance if you ensure, before you sign the contract, that you know exactly how the publisher proposes to produce, distribute and publicise your book. When you are offered a contract and advance, the publisher will almost certainly have already done some preliminary costings and sales estimates. You can ask about them.

You can also ask questions like the following: In what format will the book be published? How will it look (binding, paper and illustrations); the planned selling price; the expected first print run? Will it be issued in hardback, paperback or both? Will the hardback and paperback come out together? When will they come out? Does the publisher plan to sub-contract any rights?

It is very important to keep a note of all conversations about contracts between yourself and the publisher or agent and, of course, to keep a copy of all correspondence which can form part of a preliminary agreement and therefore can be legally binding.

You may have what appears to be the most fantastic contract and agreed terms but you should also want to know if your publisher is efficient, if their production standards are good, and if they pay over monies due promptly.

The publisher cannot guarantee sales figures but hopefully they will be closely related to the publisher's expectations.

See Sample Contract, Appendix B; Minimum Terms Agreement (MTA), Appendix D; Code of Practice, Appendix E; Sample Royalty Statement, Appendix C; See also 'Some questions authors ask' in Chapter 2

Points to Watch
Ownership of publishing house
Due to the speed of takeovers and mergers it is important to keep a close eye on who owns the publishing house and its subsidiaries and imprints; this could affect the sale of rights and royalties if your book is passed internally rather than sold. Authors may not want their book to be published by a certain company, or indeed you may have a preference for a certain imprint.

Length of copyright
The traditional practice has been that in exchange for payments the author grants to the publisher the sole and exclusive rights and licence to produce and publish the book in all languages, for the legal term of copyright (author 's life plus 50 years) throughout the world. Some authors may wish the clause to operate only while the publisher keeps the work in print. The Writers' Guild and Society of Authors suggest that this be negotiated between the publisher and author on each contract. A review after a number of years would seem to be the best compromise as the backlist is an important part of the publisher's business.

Delivery of the work
The length and delivery date of a book can affect the price, sales and marketing of books. If, for example, a book is tied to an event, there will be a rigid time schedule which the publishers have to stick to. It is important to establish as accurately as possible the nature, agreed length and scope of

the work timescale for delivery and publication of manuscript with details of illustrations, index and approximate retail price(s).

Proof corrections
Most contracts contain a clause stating that the author must bear the costs of proof corrections that exceed 10-15 per cent (excluding typesetters' errors). You should ensure that your Ms is as perfectly presented as possible when you send it to the publisher because you cannot start to improve your material at proof stage. Again, I think that with new technology and the use of computers many of these problems will evaporate. If you feel you have a genuine grievance you can of course invoke clause 16 (c) to examine the relevant parts of the publisher's accounts, as per sample contract in *Appendix B*.

Revisions (updating work)
This is a most important clause in education and technical works, especially on the death of the author. The author agrees to revise the book when requested to or to permit others to do so at the author's expense. The author and publisher should jointly decide on required revisions and, failing agreement, the question should be submitted to an arbitrator.

First option
The author may, if she so wishes, give the publisher the right of first refusal on her next book. If this clause is adapted to cover more than one work it is advisable to add, 'If however, the publishers decline the first of these works, the author shall not be bound to offer them the second.' The publisher generally undertakes to exercise this option within three months.

Moral rights
Moral rights have been enshrined in continental European copyright practice for many years. The concept of moral rights *(droit moral)* have been enshrined in the UK copyright law with the recent *Copyright, Designs and Patents Act of 1988*. They are not recognised, as yet, in Irish copyright practice

but are likely to be included in forthcoming copyright legislation. Under this law, authors of books published are provided with two basic moral rights: (a) the right of paternity (sic), whether the author is a man or woman, which guarantees that the author will be identified in any use which is made of her work, in whole or in part, and (b) of integrity, which protects the author against distortion or mutilation of her work in any adaptation or other treatment of it, both of which have the same period of duration as the period of copyright. For moral rights to be effective, a notice must be printed in the book, or at the end of an article, usually placed along with the copyright notice to say:

The right of (author's name) to be identified as the author of this work has been asserted by her in accordance with the Copyright, Designs and Patents Act 1988.

Employee works, collective works of reference, film rights and certain other works are not covered.

Most book publishers are willing to include a moral rights clause in the contract. However, authors may find that this is not so in the world of film and television.

Territories

Traditionally, the UK and USA publishers (especially general trade) have been in separate ownership and have divided and controlled the world of publishing and book selling between them. The UK publishers have defined their territory as the Commonwealth (to include the UK, Australia, New Zealand, Ireland! and South Africa, etc), whereas the USA have tried to bring Canada into their territory. This has now changed with the inclusion of English-language European rights taking the place of sole UK rights. So if an Irish publisher, for example, is buying rights from a USA publisher they will now insist on purchasing English-language European rights which includes all European countries including England. Attempts are still made by some publishers to revert to the old order.

Royalties

The amount of money an author makes from her book in royalties is dependent on what the publisher gets for the book from the public via the bookseller. Many books never yield enough sales to cover the advance paid.

Advance payment

When an advance is paid to an author it must first be made up for in sales before further money is paid out. The astute publisher will attempt to balance the advance against projected sales. The advance should not be more than the estimated sales. Unfortunately it has now become the norm rather than the exception that many books do not earn anything near as much as the publisher has paid out in the form of an advance. It is not just a question of the publisher not getting her sums right, rather a reflection of the changing nature of the industry with books now fast achieving the same shelf life as magazines - if they don't sell within a month they are returned. The vast increase in the number of books for sale is also a factor of course.

The standard practice for many years has been that the advance originally paid by the publisher to the author is set against all sums due under the contract. This means that the author receives no extra payment until the advance has been earned, whether by royalties on the original edition or from the author's share of subsidiary rights, or a combination of the two. For example, let's say that the publisher has paid an advance of £500 and has sold subsidiary rights for the sum of which the author's share is £250. £250 of the original advance has been earned, but that money will not be paid to the author, nor will any further sums be payable until the remaining £250 of the advance has been earned. This is quite fair because the publisher frequently takes into account her expectations of receipts from subsidiary rights when calculating how much the original advance should be. If the author's advance has been earned the publisher should pass to the author her share of any money received from subsidiary rights at the end of the next royalty accounting period (usually twice yearly).

The level of advance, whether it is £50, £500 or £2,000 is

based on the publisher's knowledge of the expected and potential sales of the book and bears no relation to the level of effort the publisher will make to promote it. The publisher, on signing a contract, has committed the company to spending substantial sums on producing the book. As for any other book on its list, the press will work as hard as possible to recoup its outlay, which is a guarantee of effort and interest for the author. If a book 'takes off' and unexpectedly becomes a 'bestseller', the advance seems small in terms of the sales. This will be reflected in the author's first royalty statement. She may expect a cheque for the amount exceeding her advance in the following pay-out period.

Royalty Payment
While computerisation has improved the accuracy of royalty statements, it cannot solve all the problems in this area. Estimating up-to-date royalty statements is a complex procedure dependent on several sources for information, eg sales reports from distributors all over the world, other publishers to whom rights have been sold, payment from the trade and also the high levels of returns.

Authors should check their royalty statements carefully, because of course publishers can make mistakes. There is usually a three month waiting period between the issue of statement and payment to an author and this is when any discrepancies should be sorted out.

A percentage of the sales, usually 20%, is deducted from monies owed on the royalty statement, as a protection to the publisher against 'sale or return'. The basis on which wholesalers trade with the booksellers is that a publisher sends out books as 'sales', yet the booksellers have the right to return, for credit, any copies they have not sold after a given period. The publisher must issue the bookseller with a credit note. The author's first royalty statement could show sales of say 1,000 copies and by the time the second royalty statement has issued the publisher may have received back 500 copies of the book. The publisher never asks the author to return money that the company has paid out (and this is something that is rarely referred to!).

Because of its detail, a royalty statement can be difficult to follow. Most publishers now give a statement every six months; you will receive your payment three months after this date. The gap is necessary for cash-flow purposes and for payments to come in. It also gives time for authors and publishers to sort out any queries so that you can be paid the correct amount of money. Maybe the time will come when royalties will be paid quarterly, although in most cases, payment would be quite small.

By this time you, of course, will be working on your second or even on your third book!

7 Copyright

Assigning Copyright

Copyright law is very complicated, but luckily most authors need to know only certain basic facts which I have set out below. If you need more detailed advice I suggest you contact the Society of Authors or the Writers' Guild.

Copyright automatically belongs to the creator of the original work, whether it is published or unpublished, so long as it is committed to paper. No formal process, either legal or by registration, is required to establish copyright, except in the USA where a formal deposit must be made in the Library of Congress. Some authors feel it is useful to establish the date of the work's completion by depositing a copy of it with a bank, for example, and obtaining a dated receipt.

It is usual for publishers to make the following statement (declaration) on behalf of the author in the preliminary pages of the book, to secure protection in all countries which are signatories to the Universal Copyright Convention (over sixty nations) which came into existence in the 1950s:

© copyright author's name, year of publication.

Copyright, like a patent or trademark, is a form of intellectual or creative property which can be sold, licensed, given away or bequeathed. Copyright provides protection for original writings (including computer programmes), music, recordings, films, art, sculpture and photography. Without the protection of copyright, authors would not be able to grant this exclusive right and could not demand payment for their efforts. Publishers would not risk publishing a book which, if successful, could be instantly copied by competitors. Copyright stimulates innovation and protects the author's reputation. It is also true, of course, that were it not for copyright most authors would not have the incentive to be creative because without it there would be total freedom for literary or academic works to be reproduced and exploited in a variety of ways without any obligations to recognise the interests or rights of the author.

Copyright, then, is really a property. You can assign (surrender) your copyright to another person or company but no one has the right to take it away from you or use it for their own purpose without your permission for as long as the copyright lasts. According to law, copyright lasts for the lifetime of the author plus fifty years after her death, or in the case of a work published after the author's death, for fifty years after the date of first publication. Obviously, after your death the copyright becomes part of your estate and if you don't name a specific person in your will it passes to your residual legatee. I have found that authors frequently think that they are handing over the copyright of their work to the publisher when in fact they are handing over only the right to manufacture and sell their work in a particular form.

Unless there are very special reasons for doing so, you should never surrender (assign) the copyright of your work, but instead you can grant your publisher a licence to reproduce your work, in exchange for royalty payments. This licence takes the form of a contract which, for a limited period (anything from twenty years to the full legal term of copyright), will ensure that all rights revert to you in due course if the publishers should fail to carry out the commitments of the agreement.

In the world of publishing, the 'work', as it is called, includes not only text but also diagrams, illustrations and cover design. Reproduction means not only the right to produce the work in book format but can also mean the right to sell on (sub-licence) part or all of the protected work to another publisher or company, for serialisation, adaptation, extracts, translation, film, performance, or broadcasting and so on.

Since the 1980s the Society of Authors and the Writers' Guild have sought changes around a limited period of copyright licence of, say, twenty years, only to be met by considerable resistance from publishers. However, with the shelf life of books getting shorter and shorter I cannot see why it is not possible to reach a compromise on this.

If you assign the copyright your work you lose all subsequent rights to your work in favour of the assignee for the designated period. If a publisher has bought the copyright in your book, or indeed your employer as part of your contract, they are free to edit it, change it, abridge it or do anything they like with it, without consulting you or paying you any more money. Writers who are employed on a freelance basis to produce a specific piece of work, for example journalists or report writers, are often obliged to surrender their copyright as a condition of their hire. You should *never* do this unless it is absolutely necessary and is accompanied by solid advantages.

There are some circumstances in which a publisher may justifiably wish to buy the copyright in your work, usually offering an outright fee. The fee is frequently larger than the author might expect to receive as an advance against royalties, and many authors find this acceptable so long as the fee is adequate. Some books, and indeed pamphlets, are published on this basis, for example, collections of essays or stories where an editor has to be paid and each author receives a fixed fee in exchange for a specific piece.

The editor of a collection of articles or of a reference book may be able to retain copyright in some aspect (for example, editorial organisation or structure), but it is often simplest if the publisher or a related institution takes copyright for this kind of book. Contributors to edited volumes and reference books are almost always asked to assign their copyright to the publisher. This allows single collective registration of copyright in the USA and simplifies negotiations for translation or other right sales. If you are required to assign copyright to the publisher, you should ask to retain the right to re-use your contribution (without charge or permission) in subsequent books of your own.

The assignment of copyright (in many cases for no fee) is relatively common in educational and academic publishing. Although this is regarded by some authors and publishers as invidious, academic publishers argue that they have good practical reasons for doing it. An example is where the original author of a textbook has died and successive editors have been paid to revise the book over the years, or where it is necessary to consult hundreds of contributors to a major reference work, or where financial investment can be massive. Such books can face an especially competitive market, the sale of rights can help to offset these costs. Of course, it's also true that many academics are prepared to publish without financial reward in order to disseminate their research and/or to further their professional careers.

However, in general trade publishing a mixture of the above can also be frequently found where the author retains copyright but the publisher pays a fee and can sell on the piece or reproduce it. In the case of highly illustrated, tightly laid-out books produced by 'package' publishers, the author works on much the same basis as the book designer, editor or illustrator, they are paid a fixed fee.

A word of caution. In many countries, especially in the Far East, copyright is ignored and pirate publishers abound, publishing books from Europe and America without authorisation or of course payment of royalties. Economic development policies have also encouraged pirating with one of the most obvious examples being the rise in book prices in 'developed' countries which has put books (particularly school and university textbooks) increasingly beyond the reach of poorer countries.

Permissions

Do remember that just as laws of copyright protect you, they also protect other authors and you cannot infringe their rights any more than they can yours. Permission to quote from an author should be sought, usually via their publisher, as follows:

For **prose**
(a) any extract of 400 words or more
(b) a series of extracts totalling more than 800 words
(c) a series of extracts of which any one extract is more than 300 words
(d) an extract or series of extracts comprising one-quarter of the work or more.

For **poetry**
(a) an extract of 40 lines or more
(b) a series of extracts totalling more than 40 lines
(c) an extract comprising one-quarter or more of a complete poem
(d) a series of extracts comprising together one-quarter or more of a complete poem.

Many publishers and authors will make no charge for quotations. Basic common sense and courtesy would suggest that permission is always sought and cleared. It is important however that full citation is given to the title of the extract used with the title of the work, publisher and year of publication.

Written permission to use any copyright material (text and illustrations, photographs, diagrams, maps, etc) not original to the author is required. It is the author's responsibility to obtain and pay for copyright, unless otherwise agreed — the publisher may agree to contribute, for example, £250 towards these costs for all languages and editions which are the subject of the agreement. If however the publisher pays, by agreement with the author, the author reimburses the publisher. If an index is required and the author does not wish to undertake this task, the costs shall be shared equally, the author's share to be deducted from money due to the author.

Many editors provide clearance forms to the author and insist that the forms are completed before the work goes finally to press.

Copyright deposit copies
In Ireland the publisher of every book first published must, within one month of publication deliver thirteen copies of the book to the following agencies:
1. Irish National Library, Dublin
2. British Library, London
3. National University of Ireland, Dublin (4 copies for: UCD, UCC, UCG, Maynooth)

4. The Irish Copyright Agency (5 copies for: Cambridge University Library, the Bodelian Library in Oxford, the National Library of Scotland, the National Library of Wales and Trinity College, Dublin)
5. Dublin City University, Glasnevin
6. University of Limerick

It should be pointed out that this is a highly sensitive and contentious issue within the publishing industry in Ireland, for two reasons: If a book costs £15 and you have to give away 13 free copies plus cost of P&P, this expense is considerable. The deposit centres are usually universities and therefore not open to the 'public' like say national libraries, therefore defeating the purpose of deposit in the first place.

British publishers fulfil their legal obligations by sending five copies of each of their publications to A T Smail, 100 Euston St. London NW1 2HQ for the British Library, the Bodelian Library in Oxford, Cambridge Unversity Library, the National Library of Scotland, the National Library of Wales and Trinity College, Dublin.

New technology
The development of various new technologies has had an important impact on publishing generally and on copyright in particular. Photocopying, film, television, videotapes, microfiches, computer software and on-line databases are of direct relevance to the publishing industry since all could take as their source a literary or academic work. It has been necessary for successive copyright Acts to take these new developments into account in order to maintain copyright protection.

A good publisher will ensure that the contract covers not only rights which exist now but also those which may come into existence in the future.

8 Libel and Censorship

Libel

All publishers are very well aware of the damage of libel. The publication of material which can be proven to be damaging to a person's reputation is going to be a costly matter to the publisher. Hence the growing concern in this area. If you are writing a work of non-fiction, with a controversial angle to it, your publisher will want to have it checked out for libel. Included in the author's contract (*see Appendix B*) are details of warranties which refer to the author's responsibilities in areas such as ownership of work, infringement of any existing copyright, libel, and decency. The author, by signing the contract, indemnifies the publisher against all actions, claims and costs.

The publisher reserves the right to request the author to alter or amend the text in such a way as appears appropriate, and to remove any offending passage, following legal advice.

The first and foremost responsibility must rest, in fiction and non-fiction alike, with the author. The author alone commits to paper the words which the publisher pays to publish. There is no moral justification in moving the burden of care to the publisher, although, as the book goes through the press, the publishers will often carry most of the financial burden of minimising the risk, and if a claim for libel is made the publisher will often help the author to meet her obligation. Publishers, printers, distributors and sellers of the work (including supermarkets) may be held joint or severally responsible with the author for the libel.

Censorship in Ireland

Historically, The Censorship of Publications Act, 1929 came into being after the establishment of the Irish Free state in 1922. The Act superseded the British inherited Obscene Publications Act of 1857 (still in operation in Northern Ireland) and the Customs Consolidation Act 1876. The new leadership, under the iron fist of the Irish Catholic Church, felt that a new censorship law was required to protect the Irish people from British publishers, in particular their newspapers and periodicals, as these publishers were outside the jurisdiction of the Irish courts. Ironically, under the old Act prosecution for obscenity in books was a matter for judge and jury.

The Catholic Church's obsession in Ireland with national purity, sexual repression and pandering to the middle classes encouraged public as well as private censorship, with vigilantes burning not only books but English newspapers because of their coverage of divorce cases, further repressing and restricting the freedom of individuals. Many of the major literary works of the twentieth century have been banned in Ireland, including works by Christina Stead, Jean Paul Sartre, Nadine Gordimer and James Baldwin.

It would appear that literary censorship is practised less frequently in Ireland today compared with the onslaught that began in the 1940s with, for example, the banning of Kate O'Brien's *Land of Spices* because it inferred a homosexual affair. Anthropology then became the 'in' flavour with the banning of three works by Margaret Meade. The Board again shifted their target to concentrate on Irish writers such as Edna O'Brien (1960s), then Liam O'Flaherty and Lee Dunne (who holds the honour for being the author of the last Irish book banned (1988).

'Official' censorship in Ireland, now sixty years of age, remains today in the name of The Censorship of Publications Board with only two modifications since the original Act was introduced – one with the establishment of an appeals Board (1946) and secondly in (1967) limiting the ban period on books to twelve years. With the Act has survived a censorship mentality that has serious consequences for human rights particularly in the areas of abortion, divorce and homosexuality which are still outlawed in Ireland.

The Act was further weakened on two occasions. In 1979 the Health (Family Planning) Act prohibited literature dealing with abortion and over-ruled the authority of the Censorship Board. In 1988 the Supreme Court upheld the ban on Family Planning Clinics providing information on abortion facilities in Britain.

The Censorship Act remains now 'officially' and principally to ban pornography and information on abortion. It may be invoked arbitrarily at any time as it has been with the banning of *The Joy of Sex* in 1987, for example. Books with a homosexual content have become the target of Irish censorship, eg *The Gay World* in the 1970s.

In the past twelve years the Board has concentrated its harassment on international figures such as Angela Carter, Susan Sontag, Anais Nin and Monique Wittig, thereby forbidding any cross cultural exchange.

The censorship mentality in Ireland has proved a divisive force, giving rise to ignorance and parochialism and isolating the activists and intellectuals who find themselves unable to contribute effectively to Ireland's social, political, economic and cultural life.

It is very difficult to reconcile the Censorship Board's role or its procedures with Ireland's constitutional and international commitments to freedom of expression or with its reputation abroad as a haven for cultural activity.

The United Nations (UN) organisation: Article 19, the International Centre on Censorship, was founded in 1986 and is a human rights organisation that campaigns on behalf of the right to freedom of expression worldwide. It is independent of governments, political ideologies and religious beliefs and takes its name from the nineteenth article of the Universal Declaration of Human Rights, 1948, which proclaims freedom of opinion and expression as an individual human right.

Article 19's offices are located at 90 Borough High Street, London SE1 1LL (01) 403 4822 and in Ireland, c/o TCD, Dublin 2.

Appendix A

Publishing Houses and Organisations

Irish Book Publishers

Anna Livia Press
5 Marine Road,
Dun Laoghaire
Co. Dublin
Tel: (01) 2803211
Fax: (01) 2805127
General

Anvil Books
45 Palmerston Road, Dublin 6
Tel: (01) 973628
Irish history, social history,
folklore, biography

Appletree Press
19-21 Alfred St,
Belfast BT2 8DL
Tel: (080232) 243074
Fax: (080232) 246756
International cookery books,
photographic, folklore, guidebooks

Attic Press
4 Upr Mount Street, Dublin 2
Tel: (01) 616128
Fax: (01) 616176
Books by and about women on
social and political comment,
fiction (adult and teenage), history,
women's studies, humour,
reference guides and handbooks

Avelbury Ltd
56 Sth William St, Dublin 2
Tel: (01) 6796635/6
Fax: (01) 6792973
Educational

Beaver Row Press
9 Beaver Row,
Donnybrook, Dublin 4
Tel: (01) 2695398
Poetry, short stories, special
interest

Berwick Publications
Mount Russell Cottage
Ballyconnell
Co. Cavan
Tel: (049) 26544
Cookery books

Blackstaff Press
3 Galway Park, Dundonald,
Belfast BT16 OAN
Tel:(080232) 487161
Fax (080232) 489552
Fiction, politics, history, poetry

Boole Press
26 Temple Lane
Dublin 2
Tel: (01) 6797655
Fax: (01) 6792469
Scientific, technical, medical and
scholarly

Bord na Gaeilge,
7 Cearnóg Mhuirfean
Baile Atha Cliath 2
Tel: (01) 763222
Fax: (01) 616564
Irish language literature and poetry

Brandon Book Publishers
Cooleen, Dingle Co. Kerry
Tel: (066) 51463
Fax: (066) 51234
Biography, literature, politics,
fiction, travel (Ireland), history,
folklore

Butler Sims
55 Merrion Square, Dublin 2
Tel: (01) 610614
Fax: (01) 610615
Reprints Irish and general titles

Butterworth (Ireland)
16 Upper Ormond Quay,
Dublin 7
Tel: (01) 731555
Fax: (01) 731876
Legal & Tax

**Careers & Educational
Publishers**
Lower James Street,
Claremorris, Co. Mayo
Tel: (094) 62093
Fax: (042) 35705
*Career guidance, audio-visual aids,
cookery*

The Children's Press
45 Palmerston Road, Dublin 6
Tel: (01) 973628
*Children's fiction (Irish and
historical) and illustrated books*

CITIS
2 Rosemount Terrace,
Booterstown Ave, Blackrock,
Co. Dublin
Tel: (01) 2886227
Fax: (01) 2885971
Engineering

Clavis Press
Block 4, Pye Centre, Dundrum,
Dublin 14
Tel: (01) 2988055/2988016
Fax: (01) 2988208
Trade/Technical

Cló Iar-Chonnachta Teo
Indreabchán, Co na Gaillimhe
Fón: (091) 93307
Fax: (091) 93362
Irish language textbooks and music

An Clóchomhar Teo
13 Gleann Carraig,
Baile Atha Cliath 13
Fón: (01) 324906
Irish language books

Cló Morainn
32 Ascaill Sydney, An Charraig
Dhubh, Co. Bhaile Atha Cliath
Fón: (01) 2880541
Irish language books

Clodhanna Teo
6 Sráid Fhearchair,
Baile Atha Cliath 2
Fón: (01) 783814
13 Paráid na Díge, Corcaigh
*Irish language, textbooks, short
stories, poetry, plays, novels*

Coiscéim
127 Bóthar na Trá, Dumhach
Trá, Baile Atha Cliath 4
Tel: (01) 2691889

The Columba Press
93 The Rise, Mount Merrion
Blackrock, Co. Dublin
Tel: (01) 2832954
Fax: (01) 2883770
Religious (catholic) books

Cork University Press (CUP)
University College, Cork
Tel: (021) 276871
Fax: (021) 275948
Academic

Country House *see* Town House

The Dedalus Press
24 The Heath, Cypress Downs,
Dublin 6W
Tel: (01) 902582
Poetry

Dominican Publications
42 Parnell Square, Dublin 1
Tel: (01) 731355
Fax: (01) 731760
Religious (catholic), third world

**Dublin Institute for Advanced
Studies** (School of Celtic
Studies)
10 Burlington Road, Dublin 4
Tel: (01) 680748
Fax: (01) 680561
*Irish, Celtic and Hiberno-Latin
texts*

Dundalgan Press (W Tempest)
Francis Street, Dundalk,
Co. Louth
Tel: (042) 35376
Fax: (042) 32351
Irish historical, architectural

Eason Publishing
66 Middle Abbey Street,
Dublin 1
Tel: (01) 730477
Fax: (01) 730620
Irish interest

Edmund Burke Publishers
27 Priory Drive
Blackrock, Co. Dublin
Tel: (01) 2882159

Educational Company of Ireland
Ballymount Road, Walkinstown,
Dublin 12
Tel: (01) 500611
Fax: (01) 500993
Educational textbooks

Environmental
17 Duke Street
Dublin 2
Tel: (01) 6797558

Euromedia Ltd
58 Upr Grand Canal Street,
Dublin 4
Tel: (01) 608866 Fax: (01) 684954
Trade, educational

Exemplar Publications
4 Baltrasna, Ashbourne,
Co. Meath
Tel: (01) 350663
Educational books

CJ Fallon
PO Box 1054, Lucan Road,
Palmerston, Dublin 20
Tel: (01) 6265777
Fax: (01) 6268225
School textbooks

Field Day
Foyle Arts Centre,
Old Foyle College,
Lawrence Hill, Derry BT48 7NJ
Tel: (080504) 360196
Fax: (080504) 365419
Academic, theatre, poetry, plays

Fitzwilliam Publishing Company
18 Fitzwilliam Square, Dublin 2
Tel: (01) 614575
Children's illustrated story books, folklore and history

Flyleaf Press
4 Spencer Villas, Glenageary,
Co. Dublin
Tel: (01) 2806228
Family history, natural history

Folens & Co.
8 Airton Road, Tallaght,
Dublin 24
Tel: (01) 515519 Fax: (01) 515308
School textbooks

Forum Publications
Cunabaha, Cloghroe
Blarney, Co. Cork
Tel: (021) 385798

Four Courts Press
Kill Lane, Blackrock,
Co. Dublin
Tel: (01) 2892922
Fax: (01) 2893072
Theology and religious subjects

Friars Bush Press
24 College Park Avenue,
Belfast BT7 1LR
Tel: (080232) 327695
History, photographic, architectural

The Friendly Press
61 Newtown Road
Newtown
Co. Waterford

The Gallery Press
Loughcrew, Oldcastle,
Co. Meath
Tel: (049) 41779
Fax: (049 41779
Poetry, plays by Irish authors

Gill & Macmillan
Goldenbridge, Inchicore,
Dublin 8
Tel: (01) 531005
Fax: (01) 541688
*Educational, academic, theology,
history, religion, philosophy*

The Goldsmith Press
Newbridge, Co. Kildare
Tel: (045) 33613
Irish interest, poetry, art

Grolier International
20 Parnell Square
Dublin 1
Tel: (01) 749215
Educational

An Gúm
44 Sr Uí Chonaill Uacht,
Baile Atha Cliath 1
Tel: (01) 734700
Fax: (01) 731140
*Irish language, dictionaries,
textbook, music*

Institute of Irish Studies
Queen's University Belfast,
8 Fitzwilliam Street, Belfast
Academic

**Institute of Public
Administration** (IPA)
Vergemount Hall, Clonskeagh,
Dublin 6
Tel: (01) 2697011
Fax: (01) 2698644
Economics, sociology, law

Irish Academic Press
Kill Lane, Blackrock, Co. Dublin
Tel: (01) 2892922
Fax: (01) 2893072
Academic and law

**Irish Management Institute
(IMI)**
Sandyford Road,
Dublin 16
Tel: (01) 6956911
Fax: (01) 6955150
*Management practice and
economics*

The Irish Times Collection
General Services Dept.
11-16 D'Olier Street, Dublin 2
Tel: (01) 6792022
Fax: (01) 6797991
Irish interest, humour

The Kavanagh Press
Newbridge, Co. Kildare
Tel: (045) 33613
Irish interest, Irish history, art

Kildanore Press
2 Herbert Crescent
Blanchardstown
Dublin 15
Tel: (01) 210526/210328
Fax: (01) 8210328
Religious, general and children

Libra House
4 St Kevin's Terrace,
Dublin 8
Tel: (01) 542717 Fax: (01) 546371
Trade, transport and travel

Lilliput Press
4 Rosemount Terrace, Arbour
Hill, Dublin 7
Tel: (01) 711647
Autobiography, literary criticism

Linen Hall Library
17 Donegall Square North,
Belfast BT1 5GD
Tel: (080232) 321707
Fax: (080232) 438586
Irish and local studies

Mentor Publications
Zion Road, Rathgar
Dublin 6
Tel: (01) 977621/977821

Mercier Press
PO Box No. 5,
5 French Church Street, Cork
Tel: (021) 275040
Fax: (021) 274969
*Irish folklore, music, history, travel,
theology, law*

M O Books
12 Magennis Place,
Dublin 2
Tel: (01) 719896/719584
Vulgar verse and rowdy rhymes

Monarch Line
32 Booterstown Avenue
Co. Dublin
Tel: (01) 2831336
Poetry and theatre

Morrigan Book Co
Killala,
Co. Mayo
Tel: (969) 32288
*Local history, heritage and
environment*

Moytura Press
4 Arran Quay, Dublin 7
Tel: (01) 722373 Fax: (01) 723902
General and Irish interest

National Gallery Publications
Merron Square West, Dublin 2
Tel: (01) 615133 Fax: (01) 615372

National Library of Ireland
Kildare Street, Dublin
Tel: (01) 618811
Fax: (01) 766690

Oak Tree
4 Arran Quay, Dublin 7
Tel: (01) 723923 Fax: (01) 723902
Professional and student texts

**O'Brien Educational /O'Brien
Press**
20 Victoria Road, Rathgar,
Dublin 6
Tel: (01) 979598
Fax: (01) 979274
*Educational, general Irish interest,
children, historical, architectural*

Odell & Adair
17 Lombard Street West
Dublin 8
Tel: (01) 537142 Fax: (01) 527292
Modern Irish and European fiction

Oisín Publications
4 Iona Drive,
Dublin 9
Tel: (01) 305236
Fax: (01) 307860
Sport, diaries and guidebooks

Paraclete Press
169 Booterstown Avenue,
Co. Dublin
Tel: (01) (01) 2881789
Religious (catholic)

Poolbeg Press
Knocksedan House, Forrest
Great, Swords, Co. Dublin
Tel: (01) 8407433
Fax: (01) 8403753
*Contemporary novels, short stories,
history, politics, children*

Publishing Group South West
Allihies, Bantry, Co. Cork
Tel: (027) 73025
Philosophy, short stories, children

Relay
Tyone, Nenagh,
Co. Tipperary
Tel: (067) 31734
Local history, reference

Round Hall Press
Kill Lane, Blackrock,
Co. Dublin
Tel: (01) 2892922
Fax: (01) 2893072
Law

Royal Dublin Society (RDS)
Ballsbridge, Dublin 4
Irish history, science and biology

Royal Irish Academy
19 Dawson Street,
Dublin 2
Tel: (01) 762570 Fax: (01) 762346
Sciences, Celtic studies

Sáirséal O Marcaig
13 Br Chríoch Mhór, Glasnaíon
Baile Atha Cliath 11
Tel: (01) 378914
Irish language

Salmon Publishing
The Bridge Mills,
Galway
Tel: (091) 62587
Fax: (091) 65825
Poetry

School and College Publishing
Taney Road, Dundrum,
Dublin 14
Tel: (01) 2983544
Fax: (01) 2988554
Educational books

Spellbound Books
6 Crow Street, Dublin 2
Tel: (01) 771974
Fax: (01) 6796997
Postcards

Sporting Books
4 Sycamore Road,
Mount Merrion, Co. Dublin
Tel: (01) 2887914
Sport

TEAGASC
19 Sandymount Avenue,
Dublin 4
Tel: (01) 688188
Fax: (01) 688023
Scientific manuals and journals

Topaz Publications
10 Haddington Lawn,
Glenageary, Co. Dublin
Tel: (01) 2800460
Law texts

Town House and Country House
42 Morehampton Road,
Donnybrook
Dublin 4
Tel: (01) 683307
Fax: (01) 607008
Wildlife, natural history, biography, children, fiction, art

Ulster Historical Foundation
12 College Square East,
Belfast BT1 6DD
Tel: (080232) 332288
Fax: (080232) 239888
Ulster and Irish history

Veritas Publications
Veritas House,
7-8 Lr Abbey Street, Dublin 1
Tel: (01) 788177 Fax: (01) 786507
Religious (catholic)

Watergate Press
32 Darling Street,
Enniskillen, Co. Fermanagh
Tel: (080365) 322275
Fax: (080365) 327231
Non-fiction

Wolfhound Press
68 Mountjoy Square,
Dublin 1
Tel: (01) 740354
Fax: (01) 720207
Literary studies and criticism, fiction, art, children's law

Women's Community Press see
Spellbound Books

Woodtown Music Publications
Dame House, Dame Street,
Dublin 2
Tel: (01) 6793664
Music

British Book Publishers

Please consult the following for a more comprehensive list of publishers:
Writers' and Artists' Yearbook, Cassell's Directory of Publishing, The Writer's Handbook, The Radical Bookseller Directory, Small Press Yearbook

Abacus *see* Little, Brown

Addison & Wesley
Finchampsted Road,
Wokingham, Berks, RG11 2NZ
Tel: (734) 794000
Fax: (734) 794035

Adlib *see* Scholastic Publications

Allison & Busby *see* Virgin

W H Allen *see* Virgin

Allen & Unwin *see* News Corp.

Anvil Press Poetry
69 King George Street,
London SE10 8PX
Tel (81) 858 2947
Poetry.

E & J Arnold *see* Thomson

Edward Arnold *see* Hodder & Stoughton

Aquarian Press *see* News Corp.

Ark *see* Thomson

Arkana *see* Pearson

Armada *see* News Corp.

Arrow Crime *see* Random Century

The Athlone Press
1 Park Avenue,
London NW11 7SG
Tel: (81) 458 0888
Anthropology, art, archaeology, architecture, music, religion, Science, sociology

Bantam *see* Bertelsman

Bertelsman Publishers
61-63 Uxbridge Road,
London W5 5SA
Tel: (81) 579 2652
Fax: (81) 579 5479
General Trade

A & C Black
35 Bedford Row,
London WC1R 4JH
Tel: (71) 2420946
Fax: (71) 831 8478
Arts, crafts, drama, reference, theatre, travel

Black Swan *see* Bertelsman

Blackwell Publishers
108 Cowley Road,
Oxford OX4 1JF
Tel: (865) 791100
Fax: (865) 791347
Economics, academic, social policy and administration, theology, business studies

Bloodaxe Books
PO Box 1SN,
Newcastle upon Tyne
NE99 1SN
Tel: (91) 232 5988
Poetry, literary criticism, biography, drama, photography

Bloomsbury Publishers
2 Soho Square,
London W1V 5DE
Tel: (71) 494 2111
Fax: (71) 434 0151
Trade and mass market paperbacks, reference travel, biography, fiction

Bodley Head *see* Random Century

Boxtree *see* Reed Elsevier

Boyars, Marion
24 Lacy Road,
London SW15 1NL
Tel: (81) 788 9522
Fax: (81) 789 8122
Fiction, sociology, music, travel, drama, cinema

Brimax Books *see* Reed Elsevier

Butterworths *see* Reed Elsevier

Calder Publications
9-15 Neal Street,
London WC2H 9TU
Tel: (71) 497 1741
European, international and British fiction, plays, art, literary, music and social criticism

Cambridge University Press (CUP)
The Edinburgh Building,
Shaftesbury Road,
Cambridge CB2 2RU
Tel: (223) 31293
Fax: (223) 315052
Archaeology, art, architecture, education, history, music, religion

Jonathan Cape *see* Random Century

Carcanet Press
208 Corn Exchange Buildings,
Manchester M4 3BQ
Tel: (61) 834 8730
Poetry, biography, memoirs (literary), fiction

Cassell
Villiers House, 41-47 Strand,
London WC2N 5JE
Tel: (71) 839 4900
Fax: (71) 839 1804
Academic, general non-fiction, sport, business

Century Publishing *see* Random Century

Centerprise Publishing Project
136 Kingsland High Street,
London E8 2NS
Tel: (71) 254 9632 Ex. 20/21
Community, working-class writings

W & R Chambers
43-45 Annandale Street
Edinburgh EH7 4AZ
Tel: (31) 5574571

Chapman, Geoffrey *see* Cassell

Chapman & Hall *see* Thomson

Chatto & Windus *see* Random Century

Clarendon Press *see* Oxford University Press

Robin Clark *see* Quartet Narmara

Collins *see* News Corp.

Constable & Co
3 The Lanchesters,
162 Fulham Palace Road,
London W6 9ER
Tel: (81) 741 3663
Fax: (81) 748 7562
Fiction and General Non Fiction

Leo Cooper *see* Reed Elsevier

Corgi *see* Bertelsman

Coronet *see* Hodder & Stoughton

Croom Helm *see* Thomson

Dell *see* Bertelsman

Dent J M & Sons *see* Orion

Deutsch, André
105-106 Great Russell Street,
London WC1B 3LJ
Tel: (71) 580 2746
Fax: (71) 631 3253
Art, fiction, history, humour, politics

Dinosaur *see* News Corp.

Doubleday *see* Bertelsman

Dragon's World
26 Warwick Way,
London SW1V 1RX
Tel: (71) 9765477

E P Dutton *see* Pearson

Ebury Press *see* Random Century

Edinburgh University Press
22 George Street,
Edinburgh, EH8 9LF
Tel: (31) 650 4218
Fax: (31) 662 0053
Academic

Elsevier *see* Reed Elsevier

Everywoman
34a Islington Green,
London N1 8DU
Tel: (71) 359 5496
Directories

Eyre & Spottiswoode *see* CUP

Faber & Faber
3 Queen Street,
London WC1N 3AU
Tel: (71) 465 0045
Fax: (71) 465 0034
High quality fiction and non-fiction, poetry

Fantail *see* Pearson

Federation of Worker Writers & Community Publishers
c/o 68 Grand Parade,
Brighton BN2 2JY
Tel: 273 571916
Community, working-class writings

Firefly *see* Wayland

Flamingo *see* News Corp.

Focal Press *see* Reed Elsevier

Fontana *see* News Corp.

Fourth Estate
289 Westbourne Grove,
London W11 2QA
Tel: (71) 727 8993
Fax: (71) 792 3176
Current affairs, literature, popular culture, design

Freeway *see* Bertelsman

Futura *see* Little, Brown

Gay Men's Press (GMP)
PO Box 247,
London N17 9QR
Tel: (81) 365 1545
Fax: (81) 365 1252
Biography, memoir, translation, health, social and political questions, poetry, literary criticism

Godfrey Cave
42 Bloomsbury Street
London WC1B 3QS
Tel: (71) 6369177

GMP Publishers
PO Box 247, London N17 9QR
Tel: (81) 365 1545
Fax: (81) 365 1252
Poetry, health, biographies, political analysis of primary interest to gay men

Gollancz, Victor *see* Cassell

Gower *see* News Corp.

Grafton *see* News Corp.

Granta *see* Pearson

Green Books
Ford House, Hartland, Bideford,
Devon EX39 6EE
Tel: (237) 441621
Ecological and spiritual

Green Print *see* Merlin Press

Harcourt, Brace, Jovanovich *see* Pan Macmillan

Robert Hale,
Clerkenwell House
45-47 Clerkenwell Greeen
London EC1R OHT
Tel: (71) 251 2661
Fax: (71) 490 4958
Adult general non-fiction

Hamish Hamilton *see* Pearson

Hamlyn Publishing *see* Reed Elsevier

HarperCollins *see* News Corp.

Harrap see W & R Chambers

Harvester Wheatsheaf *see* Simon & Schuster

Headline Book Publishing
Headline House,
79 Great Titchfield Street,
London WIP 7FN
Tel: (71) 631 1687
Fax: (71) 631 1958
General Trade

Heinemann *see* Reed Elsevier

Hippo Books *see* Scholastic

Hodder & Stoughton
Mill Road,
Dunton Green, Sevenoaks,
Kent TN13 2YA
Tel: (732) 450111
Fax: (732) 460134
General Trade

Hogarth *see* Random Century

Honno Welsh Women's Press
c/o Ailsa Craig, Heol y Cawl,
Dinas Powys, South Glamorgan
CF6 4AH
Tel: (222) 515014
*All kinds of books by, for or with
Welsh women*

Hutchinson Children's *see*
  Random Century

ICOM Co-Publications
18 Ashwin Street,
London E8 3DL
Tel: (71) 249 2837
Titles on co-op movement

Michael Joseph *see* Pearson

Journeyman Press *see*
  Pluto/Zwan

Kluwer Publishing (Law)
Croner House,
London Road, Kingston-upon-
Thames, Surrey KT2 6SY
Tel: (81) 549 1455
Law, Finance, Management

Knight *see* Hodder & Stoughton

Kogan Page
120 Pentonville Road,
London N1 9JN
Tel: (71) 278 0433
Fax: (71) 837 6348
Education, finance, business

Ladybird Books *see* Pearson

Allen Lane *see* Pearson

Lawrence & Wishart
144a Old South Lambeth Road,
London SW8 1XX
Tel: (71) 820 9281
Fax: (71) 587 0469
*Academic, humanities, politics,
culture*

Legend *see* Random Century

Lion Publishing
Peter's Way, Sandy Lane West,
Oxford OX4 5HG
Tel: (865) 747550
Fax: (865) 747568
Adult, Christian

Little Brown and Company
165 Great Dover Street
London SE1 47A
Tel: (71) 3344800
*Art, travel, cookery, fiction,
children*

Longman Group *see* Pearson

Macdonald *see* Little, Brown

McGraw-Hill
Shoppenhangers Road,
Maidenhead, Berks SL6 2QL
Tel: (628) 23432

**Macmillan Academic and
Professional Ltd**
4 Little Essex Street,
London WC2R 3LF
Tel: (71) 836 6633

Macmillan Education Ltd
Brunel Road,
Houndmills, Basingstoke,
Hants RG21 2XS
Tel: (256) 29242

Mainstream Publishers
7 Albany Street,
Edinburgh EH1 3UG
Tel: (31) 557 2959
Fax: (31) 556 8720
Political and alternative health

Mammoth *see* Reed Elsevier

Mandala *see* News Corp.

Mandarin *see* Reed Elsevier

Mansell Publishing *see* Cassell

Maxwell *see* Pan Macmillan

Merlin Press
10 Malden Rod,
London NW5 3HR
Tel: (71) 267 3399
Fax: (71) 284 3092
Green politics and environment

Methuen *see* Reed Elsevier

Mills & Boon
Eton House, 18-24 Paradise
Road, Richmond,
Surrey TW9 1SR
Tel: (81) 948 0444
Fax: (81) 940 5899
Romantic fiction

Minerva *see* Reed Elsevier

Mitchell Beasley *see* Reed
  Elsevier

John Murray
50 Albemarie Street,
London W1X 4BD
Tel: (71) 493 4361
Fax: (71) 499 1792
*Art, architecture, biography,
autbiography, fiction, travel,
educational*

New Beacon Books
76 Stroud Green Road,
London N4 3EN
Tel: (71) 272 4889

NEL (New English Library) *see*
  Hodder & Stoughton

News Corporation
77-85 Fulham Palace Road,
Hammersmith, London W6 8JB
Tel: (81) 741 7070
Fax: (81) 307 6408
*Leisure, true crime, popular
science, designer's guides*

Nexus *see* Virgin

W W Norton
10 Coptic Street,
London WC1A 1PU
Tel: (71) 323 1579
Fax: (71) 436 4553
*English and American literature,
history, biography, current affairs*

Octopus *see* Reed Elsevier

Oliver & Boyd *see* Pearson

Omnibus Press
8-9 Firth Street,
London W1V 5TZ
Tel: (71) 434 0066
Fax: (71) 439 2848

Onlywomen Press
38 Mount Pleasant,
London WC1X 0AP
Tel: (71) 837 0596
Lesbian fiction, theory and poetry

Open Letters
147 Northchurch Road
London N1 3NT
Tel: (71) 3594078

Optima *see* Little, Brown

Orbit *see* Little, Brown

Orion Publishing Group
Orion House
5 Upper St Martins Lane
London WC2H 9EA
Tel: (71) 240 3444

Osprey *see* Reed Elsevier

Owen, Peter
73 Kenway Road,
London SW5 0RE
Tel: (71) 373 5628
Fax: (71) 373 6760
Art, biography, fiction

Oxford University Press (OUP)
Walton Street, Oxford OX2 6DP
Tel: (865) 56767
Fax: (865) 56646
Illustrated non-fiction books

Paladin *see* News Corp.

Pan Macmillan
18-21 Cavaye Place
London SW10 9PG
Tel: (71) 373 6070
Fax: (71) 370 0746

Pandora *see* News Corp.

Papermac *see* Pan Macmillan

Pathfinder Press
47 The Cut, London SE1 8LL
Tel: (71) 261 1354

Pearson/Penguin
Bath Road, Harmondsworth,
West Drayton,
Middlesex, UB7 ODA
Tel: (81) 899 4000
Fax: (81) 899 4099
General Trade

George Philip *see* Reed Elsevier

Piatkus Books
5 Windmill Street,
London WIP 1HF
Tel: (71) 631 0710
Fax: (71) 436 7137
*Business, fiction, health, leisure,
fashion, beauty*

Picador Classics *see* Pan
  Macmillan

Piccolo *see* Pan Macmillan

Picture Corgi *see* Bertelsman

Piper *see* Pan Macmillan

Pitken Pictorials *see* Reed
  Elsevier

Pitman *see* Pearson

Pluto Publishing
345 Archway Road,
London N6 5AA
Tel: (81) 348 2724
Fax: (81) 348 9133
*Social & political science,
economics, history*

Polity Press
65 Bridge Street,
Cambridge CB2 1UR
Tel: (223) 324315
Fax: (223) 461385
*Social and political theory,
sociology, history, media*

Polygon *see* Edinburgh
  University Press

Puffin *see* Pearson

Purnell *see* Simon & Schuster

Quartet (Namara)
27-29 Goodge Street,
London WIP 1FD
Tel: (71) 636 3992
Fax: (71) 637 1866
General Trade

Random Century Group
Random Century House,
20 Vauxhall Bridge Road,
London SW1V 2SA
Tel: (71) 973 9670
Fax: (71) 233 6058
General Trade

Red Fox *see* Random Century

**Reed Elsevier Publishing
Group**
Michelin House,
81 Fulham Road,
London SW3 6RB
Tel: (71) 581 9393
Fax: (71) 589 8419
Adult General Trade

Rider *see* Random Century

Robinson Publishing
11 Shepherd House, Shepherd
Street, London W1Y 7LD
Tel: (71) 493 1064
Fax: (71) 409 7226
General 'Trade'

Routledge *see* Thomson

Rowan *see* Random Century

Sage Publications
6 Bonhill Street,
London EC2A 4PU
Tel: (71) 374 0645
Fax: (71) 374 8741
Academic

Scarlet Press
5 Montague Road
London E8 2HN
Tel: (71) 241 3702
Fax: (71) 753 5100

Sceptre *see* Hodder & Stoughton

Scholastic Publications
Villiers House, Clarendon
Avenue, Leamington Spa,
Warks CV32 5PR
Tel: (926) 887799
Fax: (926) 883331
Children

Secker & Warburg *see* Reed
  Elsevier

Seren Books
Andmar Hse, Tondu Road,
Bridgend,
Mid-Galmorgan F31 425
Tel: (656) 767834

Serpent's Tail
4 Blackstock Mews,
London N4 2BT
Tel: (71) 354 1949
Fax: (71) 704 6467
*Literary and experimental work,
modern fiction, translations*

Sheba Feminist Press
10a Bradbury Street,
London N16 8JN
Tel: (71) 254 1590
Fax: (71) 249 5351
*Children's and writing by black
women, working class, new writers
and lesbians*

Sheldon *see* SPCK (Adult)

Sidgwick & Jackson *see* Pan
  Macmillan

Simon & Schuster
West Garden Place,
Kendal Street, London W2 2AQ
Tel: (71) 7247577

Colin Smythe,
PO Box 6, Gerrards Cross,
Bucks SL9 8XA
Tel: (753) 886000
Literary criticism, folklore, fantasy

**Society for Promoting
Christian Knowledge (SPCK)**
Holy Trinity Church,
Marylebone Road,
London NW1 4DU
Tel: (71) 387 5282
Fax: (71) 388 2352
Theology and religion

Sphere Books *see* Little, Brown

Stramullion Co-op
11a Forth Street,
Edinburgh EH1 3LE
*Feminist, fiction, poetry and non-
fiction by Scottish women*

Sweet & Maxwell *see* Thomson

Tavistock Publications *see*
  Thomson

Thomson
11 New Fetter Lane
London EC4P 4EE
Tel: (71) 583 9855
General trade

Thorsons *see* News Corp.

Times Books *see* News Corp.

Triangle *see* SPCK

Tycooly Publishing *see* Cassell

Ultra Violet Books
c/o Prism Press, 2 South Street,
Bridport, Dorset DT6 3NQ
Tel: (308) 27022
*Feminist non-fiction,
autobiography*

Unwin Hyman *see* News Corp.

Verso
6 Meard Street,
London W1V 3HR
Tel: (71) 437 3546
Politics, history, philosophy,
economics

Vintage *see* Random Century

Virago
20-23 Mandela Street,
Camden Town,
London NW1 OHQ
Tel: (71) 383 5150
Fax: (71) 383 4892
Books of general interest on all
aspects of women's lives

Virgin Publishing
26 Grand Union Centre,
338 Ladbroke Grove,
London W10 5AH
Tel: (81) 968 7554
Fax: (81) 968 0929
Adult general

Walker Books
87 Vauxhall Walk,
London SE11 5HJ
Tel: (071) 793 0909
Fax: (71) 587 1123
Children and teenagers

Wayland
61 Western Road Hove East
Sussex BN3 1 JD
Tel: (273) 722561

Ward Lock *see* Cassell

Weidenfeld George & Nicolson
see Orion

John Wiley,
Baffins Lane, Chichester,
West Sussex PO19 1UD
Tel: (243) 779777
Fax: (243) 775878
Behavioural sciences and
management

The Women's Press
34 Great Sutton Street,
London EC1V ODX
Tel: (71) 251 3007
Fax: (71) 608 1938
Books of general interest on all
aspects of women's lives

Workers Educational
Association (WEA)
Temple House, 9 Upper
Berkeley Street,
London W1H 8BY
Tel: (71) 402 5608
Adult, trade union, community
and women's education

Worldwide *see* Mills & Boon

Yearling *see* Transworld

Young Corgi *see* Bertelsman

Zed Books
57 Caledonian Road,
London N1 9BU
Tel: (71) 837 4014
Fax: (71) 833 3960
Development and environmental
studies, third world

Zwan *see* Pluto Publishing

Organisations

For more detailed and local lists consults the *Writers' and Artists' Yearbook*

AONTAS
22 Earlsfort Terrace
Dublin 2
Tel: (01) 754121

An Chomhairle Leabharlanna
(The Library Council)
53/54 Upper Mount Street,
Dublin 2 Tel: (10)

Arts Club/Authors' Club,
40 Dover Street,
London WIX 3RB

Arts Club, United Irish
3 Upper Fitzwilliam Street
Dublin 2
Tel: (01) 611411

Arts Council Irish /An
Chomhairle Ealaion
70 Merrion Square Dublin 2
Tel: (01) 611840
Fax: (01) 761302

Arts Council of Great Britain
14 Great Peter Street, London
SWIP 3NQ Tel: (71) 333 0100

Arts Council of Northern Ireland
181a Stranmillis Road,
Belfast BP9 5DU
Tel: (0232) 381591

Association of Authors' Agents
79 St Martin's Lane,
London WC2N
Tel: (71) 836 4271.

Association of Freelance Editors and Indexers
c/o 45 Eglinton Road,
Donnybrook, Dublin 4
Tel: (01) 2692214

Association of Illustrators,
1 Colville Place,
London WIP 1HN.
Tel (71) 636 4100

Association of Little Presses,
89a Petherton Road,
London N5 2QT
Tel: (71) 226 2657

Authors' Guild of Ireland Ltd
282 Swords Road, Dublin 9
Tel: (1) 375974

Authors' Licensing and Collecting Society Ltd (ALCS)
33/34 Alfred Place,
London WC1E 7DP.
Tel: (71) 255 2034

Blind Writers' Association,
32 Greenwood Avenue, Trent
Vale, Stoke-on-Trent,
Staffs ST4 6NG
Tel: (782) 658 287

Book Exchange, The
9 Elizabeth Gardens Sunbury-
on-Thames,
Middlesex, TW16 5LG

Book House Ireland
65 Middle Abbey Street
Dublin 1
Tel: (1) 730 108

Book Marketing Council The
Publishers Association
19 Bedford Square
London WC1B 3HJ

Book Packagers Association,
93a Bleheim Crescent,
London W11 2EQ.
Tel: (71) 221 9089

Book Trust (National Book
League) Book House
45 East Hill
London SW18 2QZ
Tel: (81) 870 9055
Fax: (81) 874 4790

**Booksellers' Association
Ireland,**
Book House Ireland
65 Middle Abbey Street,
Dublin 1
Tel: (01) 730108

**Booksellers' Association of
Great Britain**
272 Vauxhall Bridge Road,
London SW1V 1BA.
Tel: (71) 834 5477

British Copyright Council, The
29-33 Berners Street,
London WIP 4AA

British Fantasy Society, The
15 Stanley Road, Morden,
Surrey SM4 5DE.
Tel: (81) 540 9443
(crime, horror and related
fields)

British Guild of Travel Writers,
The Bolts Cross Cottage,
Peppard, Henley-on Thames,
Oxon RG9 5LG
Tel: (4971) 411

**British Science Fiction
Association,** The
29 Thornville Road, Hartlepool,
Cleveland TS2 8EW

**Cartoonist Club of Great
Britain,**
2 Camden Hill, Tunbridge
Wells, Kent TN2 4TH

**Censorship of Publications
Board and Censorship of
Publications Appeal Board**
13 Lr Hatch Street, Dublin 2
Tel: (01) 610553

**Chartered Society of
Designers,** The
29 Bedford Square,
London WC1B 3EG
Tel: (71) 631 1510

Children's Book Foundation,
Book House,
45 East Hill, London SW18 4QZ
Tel: (81) 870 9055

**Children's Literature
Association of Ireland**
PO Box No. 3594, Dublin 1
Tel: (01) 283 5552

**Children's Writers and
Illustrators Group**
84 Drayton Gardens
London SW10 9SB
Tel: (71) 373 6642

**CLÉ (The Irish Book
Publishers' Association)**
PO Box No. 3594, Dublin 1
Tel: (01) 283 5552

**Comedy Writers' Association
of Great Britain,**
61 Parry Road,
Wolverhampton WV11 2PS
Tel: (9020 722729

**Copyright Licensing Agency,
The (ICLA),** The
Irish Writers' Centre
19 Parnell Square Dublin 1
Tel: (01) 729090

Copyright Licensing Agency
90 Tottenham Court Road,
London WIP 9HE
Tel: (71) 436 5931

Crime Writers' Association
PO Box 172 Tring,
Herts HP23 5LP

Critics' Circle, The
47 Bermondsey Street,
London SE1 3XT
Tel: (71) 403 1818

Design and Artists Copyright Society,
St Mary's Clergy House,
2 Whitechurch Lane,
London E1 7QR.
Tel: (71) 247 1650

Folklore Society, The
c/o University College, Gower Street, London WC1E 6BT
Tel: (71) 387 5894

Freelance Editors and Proofreaders, Society of
16 Brenthouse Road,
London E9 6QG
Tel: (81) 986 4868

Freelance Photographers' Bureau
497 Green Lanes,
London N13 4BP
Tel: (81) 882 3315

Gay Authors' Workshop BM Box 5700 London WC1N 3XX

Ghost Story Society, The
2 Looe Road, Croxteth,
Liverpool L11 6LJ
Tel: (51) 546 2287

Independent Publishers' Guild, 25 Cambridge Road,
Hampton, Middlesex TW12 2JL
Tel: (81) 979 0150

Irish Academy of Letters
c/o School of Irish Studies,
PO Box 2663, Dublin 4

Irish Books Marketing Group
PO Box No. 3594, Dublin 1
Tel: (01) 283 5552

Irish Children's Book Trust
c/o PO Box No. 3594, Dublin 1
Tel: (01) 283 5552

Irish Writers' Union, The
19 Warwick Villas, Ranelagh,
Dublin 6, Tel: (01) 976 771

Irish Writers' Centre
19 Parnell Square, Dublin 1
Tel: (01) 729090

KLEAR
St Mary's School, Swan's Nest Road, Kilbarrack, Dublin 3
Tel: (01) 316255

Library Association of Ireland/
Cumann Leabharlann na hEireann
53 Upr Mount Street, Dublin 2
Tel: (01) 619000

Library Association, The
7 Ridgmount Street,
London WC1E 7AE
Tel: (71) 636 7543

Media Society, The
Church Cottage, East Rudham,
Norfolk PE31 8QZ
Tel: (485) 528664

National Poetry Foundation
27 Mill Road, Fareham,
Hants PO16 OTH.
Tel: (329) 822218

National Union of Journalists (NUJ)
Acorn House, 314 Gray's Inn Road, London WC1X 8DP.
Ireland: Liberty Hall,
Dublin 1
Tel: (01) 741207

New Playwright Trust
Whitechapel Library,
77 Whitechapel High Street
London E1 7OX

Outdoor Writers' Guild,
86 Burford Gardens,
London N13 4LP
Tel: (81) 886 1957

PEN International
(Playwrights, Poets, Editors, Essayists, Novelists)
9/10 Charterhouse Buildings,
Goswell Road,
London EC1M 7AT
Tel: (71) 253 4308

Player-Playwrights,
St Augustine's Church Hall,
Queen's Gate, London SW1

Playwrights Trust
Interchange Studios, Dalby
Street, London NS5 3NQ
Tel: (71) 284 2818

Playwrights' Co-operative, The
60/71 Collier Street,
London N1 9BE
Tel: (71) 713 7125

Poetry Society, The
24 Betterton Street,
London WC2H 9BU
Tel: (71) 240 4810

Public Lending Right Office,
Bayheath House, Prince Regent,
Street Stockton-on-Tees,
Cleveland TS18 1DF

Publishers' Association, (PA)
19 Bedford Square,
London WC1B 3HJ
Tel: (71) 580 6321 see Clé

Publishers' Licensing Society,
90 Tottenham Court Road,
London WIP 9HE
Tel: (71) 436 3986

Reading Association of Ireland
Educational Research Centre,
Drumcondra, Dublin 9
Tel: (01) 373 799

**Romantic Novelists'
Association,** The
Half Hidden, West Lane,
Bledow, Prices Risborough,
Bucks, HP17 9PF

Small Press Centre, The
Room T202, All Saints Site,
Middlesex University, White
Hart Lane, London N17 8HR
Tel: (81) 362 5000 Ext. 6058

Society of Authors, The
84 Drayton Gardens, London
SW10 9SB Tel: (71) 373 6642
Not affiliated to the TUC

Society of Indexers
38 Rochester Road,
London NW1 9JJ
Tel: (71) 916 7809

Society of Irish Playwrights,
The Room 804, Liberty Hall,
Dublin 1

Society of Women Artists,
Westminster Gallery,
Westminister Central Hall,
Storey's Gate,
London SW1H 9NU

**Society of Women Writers and
Journalists**
110 Whitehall Road, Chingford,
London E4 6DW
Tel: (81) 529 0886

Society of Young Publishers
12 Dyott Street,
London WC1A IDF

Theatre Writers' Union
4 Chenies Street,
London WC1E 7EP

Translators' Association, The
84 Drayton Gardens,
London SW10 9SB
Tel: (71) 373 6642

Tyrone Guthrie Centre, The
Annaghmakerrig House,
Newbliss, Co. Monaghan
Tel: (01) 047) 54003

Women in Publishing (WIP)
c/o Whitaker 12 Dyott Street
London WC1A 1DF

Women Writers' Network
55 Burlington Lane,
London W4 3ET
Tel: (81) 994 0598

**Workers Educational
Association** (WEA),
Temple House 9 Upper Berkeley
Street, London W1H 8BY

Writers' Guild of Great Britain
430 Edgware Road
London W21 EH

Appendix B

Sample Author Contract

Preamble
MEMORANDUM OF AGREEMENT made this 12 December, 1998

BETWEEN **(Róisín Conroy or Author's name)

Of **(Author's Address)

(hereinafter called the 'Author' or 'Editor', which expression shall, where the context admits, include the Author's/Editor's executors, administrators and assigns or successors in business as the case may be) of the one part and

ATTIC PRESS LIMITED
of 4 Upper Mount Street, Dublin 2.

(hereinafter called 'the Publishers', which expression shall, where the context admits, include any publishing imprint subsidiary to or associated with the Publishers, and the Publishers' executors, administrators and assigns or successors in business as the case may be) of the other part.

Whereby it is mutually agreed as follows concerning the undermentioned work original to the Author and provisionally entitled:

** *So You Want To Be Published*? (Working Title).
(hereinafter called 'the Work'),

Multiple Authors
If there are multiple Authors under this Agreement, the obligations of all the Authors will be joint and several unless otherwise expressly provided in this Agreement and the Publishers may exercise any or all of its remedies with respect to the Authors individually or collectively. For the purposes of this Agreement, all Authors shall be collectively referred to as the 'Author.'

1. Rights Granted
In consideration of the payments hereinafter mentioned and subject to the terms and conditions herein contained, the Author hereby grants to the Publishers the sole and exclusive right and

licence to produce and publish and themselves further to licence
the production and publication of the Work or any adaptation, or
any abridgement of the Work or any substantial part of the Work
in volume form in all languages for the legal term of the copyright
throughout the world.

2. Delivery of the Work

The complete typescript of which shall include **144 approx.
pages, or **60,000 words maximum in length and **shall be
delivered/has been delivered in duplicate or on disc and one hard
copy to the Publishers ready for the typesetter together with any
illustrations and/or other material deemed to be reasonably
necessary under the terms of this Agreement, conforming to the
specifications set out in any attached schedule of this agreement,
not later than 28 August, 2000.

Should the Author fail to deliver acceptable typescript copies and
such other material as may be specified by the Publisher of the
complete Work on the due date, other than for extraordinary
reasons mutually agreed, or by such other date as may be agreed
by the Publishers in writing, the Publishers shall be at liberty to
decline to publish the Work and this Agreement shall terminate,
subject to the following alternative provisos, the choice of which
shall be in the sole discretion of the Publishers:

(a) that the Author shall not be at liberty to publish the Work
elsewhere without having first offered the completed typescript to
the Publishers on the terms of this Agreement;
or
(b) that the Author shall refund any part of the advance already
paid by the Publishers within thirty days of a request in writing
from the Publishers to do so.

3. Acceptance and Conditions of Acceptance

The Publishers shall accept the Work provided that the complete
typescript as delivered by the Author conforms to a reasonable
extent in nature, scope and style to the specifications set out in this
Agreement; and they shall have the right as a condition of
acceptance of the Work to require amendments by the Author to
ensure that the Work does so conform. If the Author is unable or
unwilling to undertake such amendments or arrange for them to
be made within such reasonable period of time as shall have been
agreed by the Publishers, then the Publishers shall after
consultation with the Author have the right to employ a
competent person or persons to make the amendments and any

fees payable shall be deducted from any sums due to the Author under the terms of the Agreement.

4. Competing Work

The Author undertakes that she will not during the continuance of this Agreement without the written consent of the Publishers prepare, otherwise than for the Publishers, any work of a nature which may be reasonably considered by the Publishers to be likely to compete with or affect prejudicially the sales of the Work or the exploitation of any rights in the Work granted to the Publishers under this Agreement.

5. Responsibility to Publish

The Publishers shall unless otherwise mutually agreed, or unless prevented by circumstances beyond their control, produce and publish the Work at their own risk and expense in a style and manner they consider appropriate and unless prevented by circumstances outside their control within a reasonable time of acceptance of the Work, to be confirmed in writing within three months of delivery of final Work, in accordance with the terms and conditions of this Agreement.

6. Textual Copyright Materials

In respect of all copyright materials (textual extracts from other copyright works and any illustrations), the Author shall obtain from the owners of the respective copyrights written permission (which shall be forwarded to the Publishers on delivery of the material) to reproduce such material in the Work and in all territories and editions and in all forms thereof which are the subject of this Agreement.

Written permission to use any copyright material not original to the Author for which permission is required shall be obtained for all territories, languages and editions which are the subject of this Agreement by the Author who agrees to bear all fees (unless otherwise agreed) for the use of such material or promptly reimburse the Publishers for any fees paid by them in respect of such copyright materials.

7. Illustrations

If in the reasonable opinion of the Publishers and Author illustrations are desirable, the Author shall, unless otherwise mutually agreed, obtain for the Publishers' use with the written permission of the copyright owner, free of charge and copyright fee in relation to all languages and editions which are the subject of the Agreement, suitable photographs, pictures, diagrams, drawings, maps and other material for illustrating. The Publishers shall also be entitled to do so and the cost may be borne by the Author unless otherwise agreed.

All illustrations supplied by the Author shall be in a form suitable for reproduction and the Publishers shall have the right to reject such material or to require of the Author such substitutions or amendments as may, in the reasonable view of the Publishers, be required on the grounds of poor quality, excessive cost or otherwise. All illustrations, when finished with, shall be returned to the Author, if she so requests in writing.

8. Index

If in the reasonable opinion of the Publishers an index is required it shall be supplied by the Author at her own expense in typescript form within fourteen days of receipt by the Author of final page proofs. If the Author is unable to supply the index then the Publishers shall arrange for it to be done and the cost shall be deducted from the Author's earnings unless otherwise agreed.

9. Production, Promotion and Negotiation Responsibility

While proper care will be taken of the Work, the Publishers shall not be responsible for any loss or damage to it while it is in the Publishers' possession or in the course of the production or in transit. All parts of the Work supplied by the Author shall, when finished with, be returned to the Author if she so requests in writing.

The negotiations and final agreement to terms of exploitation of all rights granted under this agreement, shall be in the control of the Publishers, who shall whenever practicable consult the Author, concerning the sale of USA paperback, mass-market paperback, serial and book club rights. The Publisher shall in all other respects have the entire control of the publication.

All matters relating to the publication of the Work including the paper, design, printing, binding, jacket or cover and embellishments, the manner and extent of the promotion and advertisement, the number and distribution of free copies for the Press or otherwise, the print number, the reprinting, pricing and terms of sale of the first and any subsequent edition or impression of the Work issued by the Publishers shall be under the entire control of the Publishers. The Author shall be shown artists' roughs or proofs of the jacket cover design and shall be consulted, if the Author so requests in advance in writing, therein in good time before they are passed for press.

The Author undertakes to be available, if so requested in advance by the Publishers, to assist the Publishers in the promotion of the work.

Use of Author's Name

The Publishers undertake to set the name of the Author in its customary form with due prominence on the title page and on the binding, jacket and/or cover of every copy of the Work published by them and shall use their best endeavours to ensure that a similar undertaking is made in respect of any editions/forms of the Work licensed by them.

The Publishers may use the Author's name in the Work and all revisions thereof and in connection with the Work's advertising and promotion.

10. Authors Proofs and Corrections

The Author undertakes to read, check and correct the proofs and artwork of the Work and to return them within seven days of their receipt to the Publishers, failing which the Publishers may consider the proofs as passed for press. The cost of all additions, deletions and revisions made by the Author in the finished artwork and in the proofs (other than the corrections of artists', copy editors' or printers' errors) above 10 per cent of the original cost of composition shall be borne by the Author. Should any charge arise under this Clause the amount may be deducted from any sum which may become due to the Author under this Agreement.

11. Warranties

The Author hereby warrants to the Publishers and their assignees and licensees that: she has full power to make this Agreement that she is the sole Author of the Work and is the owner of the rights herein granted that the Work is original to her, and has not previously been published in any form in the territories covered by this Agreement; that the Work is in no way whatever a violation or an infringement of any existing copyright or licence, or duty of confidence, or duty to respect privacy, or any other right of any person or party whatsoever, that it contains nothing libellous or in breach of Official Secrets Acts or in any other way unlawful and, that all statements contained therein purporting to be facts are true and that any recipe, formula or instruction contained therein will not, if followed accurately, cause any injury, illness or damage to the user.

The Author further warrants that the Work contains no obscene or improper material.

The Author will indemnify and keep the Publishers indemnified against all actions, suits, proceedings, claims, demands, damages and costs (including any legal costs or expenses properly incurred and any compensation costs and disbursements paid by the Publishers on the advice of their legal advisers to compromise or settle any claim) occasioned to the Publishers in consequence of any breach of this warranty or arising out of any claim alleging that the Work constitutes in any way a breach of this warranty.

The Publishers reserve the right, having first notified the author, to insist that the Author amend the text of the Work in such a way as may appear to them appropriate for the purpose of modifying or removing any passage which in their absolute discretion or on the advice of the Publishers' legal advisers may be considered objectionable or likely to be actionable by law, but any such amendment or deletion shall be without prejudice to and shall not affect the Author's liability under her warranty and indemnity herein contained.

Should the work become the subject of a complaint alleging libel the decision of the Publishers as to whether or not to repudiate liability or to contest an action of proceedings ensue or to settle the claim upon such terms as they may be advised shall be final and the Author shall have no ground for action against the Publishers in respect of its implementation.

All warranties and the indemnities herein contained shall survive the termination of this Agreement.

12. Royalties and Fees Payable on Own Editions
General Proviso
Subject to the terms and conditions set out in this Agreement the Publishers shall pay to the Author the following royalties and fees in respect of all copies of the Work sold.

The Publishers reserve the right not to pay royalties or sums otherwise due to the Author until payment for the sale of copies is received by the Publishers. Any sum of money due to the Author in respect of sub-licensed rights shall be paid to the Author within three months of receipt by the Publishers provided that the advance has been earned.

No royalties shall be paid on copies of the Work sold at cost or less; presented to the Author; presented in the interests of the sale of the Work including review copies; lost through theft or damaged or destroyed by fire, water, in transit or otherwise; or on any copies returned or refunded to the Publishers for any reason.

(a) Home Hardbound/Cased Edition Sales (Retail)
On the published price of all copies sold, excluding such copies as may be sold subsequent to the provisions of this Agreement, or as otherwise mutually agreed, and subject to a different royalty: a royalty of **xxx per cent. (Rising Scale)

(b) Export and Special Discount Hardbound Sales (Wholesale)
On all copies sold at a discount of 50 per cent or more, for export
or for bulk sales at home or overseas, except as otherwise specified
in this Agreement a royalty of **xxx per cent of the net amounts
received by the Publishers. (Rising Scale)

(c) Small Reprints
On reprints of **xxxx copies or less the royalties under (a) and (b)
above shall revert to (a) and (b) respectively or to the lowest rates
provided thereunder. The Publishers may not invoke this
provision more than once in twelve months without the prior
agreement of the Author.

(d) Publishers' Hardbound Cheap Editions
On the published price of the Publishers' hardbound cheap edition
of the Work issued at two-thirds or less of the latest notified
published price of the latest edition, a royalty of **xxx per cent of
the published price on home sales and **xxx per cent of the net
amounts received by the Publishers on all copies sold for export or
wholesale excluding such copies as may be sold subsequent to the
provisions of this Agreement, or as otherwise mutually agreed.

*(e) Publishers' Own Trade Paperback Edition (Retail &
Wholesale)*
On all copies sold of the Work in paperback by the Publishers'
wholly or partly owned imprint, a royalty of not less than **xxx
per cent of the published price to **xxx,000 copies and **xxx per
cent thereafter on all copies sold on the home market and **xxx
per cent of the published price on all copies sold in the export
market and **xxx per cent of the net amounts received by the
Publishers on all copies sold at a discount of 50 per cent or more
on the home and export markets to **xxx,000 copies **xxx per cent
thereafter of the net amounts received by the Publishers.

(f) Publishers' Own Mass-Market Paperback Editions
In the event of the publication of the Work in mass-market
paperback by the Publishers or by their wholly or partially owned
imprint, a royalty of not less than *xxx per cent of the published
price to **xxx,000 copies and **xxx per cent thereafter on all copies
sold on the home market and **xxx per cent of the net amounts
received by the Publishers on all copies sold at a discount of 50 per
cent or more on the home and export market to **xxx,000 copies
**xxx per cent thereafter of the net amounts received by the
Publishers.

(g) Mail Order Sales
On all copies sold to the consumer through the medium of mail
order, coupon advertising or direct by mail circulation, a royalty of
**xxx per cent of the net receipts (excluding postage).

(h) Premium Sales

Should the Publishers with the consent of the Author, which shall not be unreasonably withheld, sell copies of the Work to be given away in connection with services or goods other than books, the sums payable to the Author shall be mutually agreed.

13. Royalties and Fees Payable on Licensed Editions

(a) Trade Paperback Editions Licensed to Another Publisher

**xxx per cent of the net amounts received by the Publishers.

(b) Mass-Market Paperback Editions Licensed to Another Publishers.

**xxx per cent of the net amounts received by the Publishers.

(c) Other Editions

On all copies sold under licence by Publishers other than those detailed herein: 50 per cent of the net amounts received by the Publishers.

(d) Royalty-Inclusive Sales

The Publisher shall make every effort to arrange for the publication of the Work in the USA, Canada, Australia, New Zealand under a royalty agreement related to the published price. Where a separate agreement is made for the publication of the Work overseas under which copies are to be supplied bound or in sheets on a royalty-inclusive basis, **xxx per cent of the net amounts received by the Publishers.

(e) Book Clubs (Wholesale)

On all copies sold to book clubs or similar organisations for sale to their members at a special published price **xxx per cent of the net amount received by the Publishers:

(i) Where the transaction between the Publishers and the book club is on a royalty basis **xxx per cent of the net amounts received by the Publishers.

(ii) Where the Publishers manufacture for the book club at a price inclusive of royalty, terms to be agreed between the parties hereto.

14. Royalties and Fees Payable on Other Licensed Rights

In consideration of the payment by the Publishers to the Author of the following percentages of all monies received by them in respect of the undermentioned rights the Author hereby grants the said rights in so far as they are not granted by Clause 1 (above) to the Publishers within the territories specified therein during the term of this Agreement.

On the sale, assignment or licensing to others of rights to all or part of the work as follows:

	Amount to Author
(a) Quotation and Extract Rights	50 per cent
(b) Anthology Rights	50 per cent
(c) Digest Rights (ie the right to publish an abridgement of the Work in a single issue of a journal, periodical or newspaper)	50 per cent
(d) Digest Book Condensation Rights (ie the right to publish a shortened form of the Work in volume form)	50 per cent
(e) One-shot Periodical Rights (ie the right to publish the complete work or any extract from it in a single issue of a journal, periodical or newspaper)	50 per cent
(f) Second and Subsequent Serial Rights (ie the right to publish one or more extracts from the Work in successive issues of a periodical or newspaper beginning at or following publication of the Publishers' first edition of the Work (in Volume form)	**xxx per cent
(g) First Serial Rights (ie the right to publish one or more extracts from the Work in successive issues of a periodical or newspaper beginning before publication of the first edition of the Work (in volume form))	**xxx per cent
(h) Foreign Publication Rights (eg USA, Canada, Australia, New Zealand).	**xxx per cent
(j) Strip Cartoon Book Rights or Picturisation Book Rights	50 per cent
(k) Translation Rights	**xxx per cent
(l) Dramatisation and Documentary Rights on stage, film, radio, television including transmission by cable, satellite or any other medium	90 per cent
(m) Single-Voice Readings (ie the right to read from the text of the Work)	75 per cent
(n) Merchandising Rights, ie the right to exploit characters, items and events in the Work through the manufacture, licensing and/or sale of goods and services, including but not limited to drawings, calendars, toys, games, novelties, figures,	

souvenirs, trinkets, fabrics, clothing, food and
drinks   **xxx per cent

(o)   (i) Mechanical Reproduction Rights (ie the right
to produce or reproduce the Work or to license the
reproduction of the Work or any part thereof by film
micrography, reprographic reproduction, gramophone
records, or tapes, film strips, or by means of any
other contrivance whether now in existence or
hereinafter invented, except in so far as reproduction
is for use as part of or in conjunction with a
commercial cinematograph film)   **xxx per cent
        (ii) Film Strip Rights (ie the right to
reproduce the Work on a film strip or loop)   50 per cent
        (iii) Electronic Publishing Rights (ie the
right to produce or to license the production
of any system or programme derived from or utilising
the Work and designed for use in electronic
information storage or retrieval systems now in
existence or hereinafter invented)   **xxx per cent

(p) Non-Commercial Rights for the Print-Handicapped
(ie the right to convert the Work to Braille or to
record it for the sole use of the blind and print-
handicapped   free of charge

15. Advance Payment
The Publishers agree to pay the Author in advance and on account
of all sums that may become due to the Author under this
Agreement the sum of IR£***000.00 payable:

IR£*00.00 on signing of contract
IR£*00.00 on receipt of and acceptance of completed MS, such
acceptance not to be unreasonably withheld.
IR£*00.00 on publication date

16. Statement of Sales
(a) The Publishers shall make up semi-annually a statement of
all sales of copies of the Work on **31 March/30 September
following the date of first publication and all monies due to the
Author shall be paid to her within three months of the said
accountancy dates. However, no accounts need be submitted
unless specifically demanded nor payment made in respect of any
year in which the sum due is less than IR£50 in which case the
amount will be carried forward to the next accountancy date.

116

(b) The Publishers shall at their discretion have the right to set aside as a reserve against returns a sum representing in the case of a hardback edition 10 per cent and in the case of a paperback edition 20 per cent of the royalties earned under Clause 12 hereof during the first six months after publication of any edition of the Work, and to withhold this sum for a period up to and including the third royalty statement following publication, after which all monies due shall be paid in full at the time of the next royalty statement

(c) The Author or her Authorised representative shall have the right upon written request to examine the records of account of the Publishers in so far as they relate to the sales and receipts of the Work, which examination shall be at the cost of the Author unless errors exceeding 10 per cent of such sales and receipts in respect of the last preceding accounting period to her disadvantage shall be found, in which case the cost shall be paid by the Publishers.

(d) Any overpayment made by the Publishers to the Author in respect of the Work may be deducted from any sums subsequently due to the Author in respect of the Work.

17. VAT
The Publishers operate a self-billing system for the payment of royalties and to account for Value Added Tax. The Publishers therefore require details of the Author's VAT registration number where applicable which shall be supplied upon signature of this Agreement. Should the Author fail to supply a VAT registration number the Publishers shall not pay VAT on any sums due under the terms of this Agreement.

18. Copyright
The copyright of the Work shall remain the property of the Author and the copyright note to be printed in every copy of the Work shall be in the Author's name, with the year of first publication.

19. Copyright Infringement
If at any time during the continuance of the Agreement the copyright of the Work in the reasonable opinion of the Publishers be infringed, and the Author after receiving written notice of such infringement from the Publishers refuses or neglects to take proceedings in respect of the infringement, the Publishers shall be entitled to take proceedings in the joint names of the Publishers and the Author upon giving the Author a sufficient and reasonable security to indemnify the Author against any liability for costs, and in this event any sum received by way of damages

shall belong to the Publishers. If the Author is willing to take proceedings and the Publishers desire to be joined with her as a party thereto and agree to share the costs, then if any sum is recovered by way of damages and costs such sum shall be applied in payment of the costs incurred and the balance shall be divided equally between the Author and the Publishers. The provisions of the clause are intended to apply only in the case of an infringement of the copyright in the Work affecting the interest in the same granted to the Publishers under this Agreement.

20. Author Free Copies
The Publishers shall give to the Author on publication **six complimentary copies of the first edition of the Work and **three complimentary copies of each subsequent edition or revised edition of the Work. The Author shall have the right to purchase at normal trade terms further copies for personal use but not for resale. The Publisher shall also send to the Author one copy of each sublicensed edition on receipt from the sublicensing Publisher.

21. Updating/Revision of Work/New Edition
(a) Should the Author and the Publishers agree that a revision of the Work is necessary, the Author shall, without charge to the Publishers, edit and revise the Work during the currency of this agreement and shall supply any new matter that may be needed to keep the Work up to date within a reasonable period. In the event of the Author neglecting or being unable for any reason to revise or edit the Work or supply new matter where needed within a reasonable period the Publishers may procure some other person to revise the Work, or supply new matter, and may deduct the expense thereof from royalties or other sums payable to the Author under this Agreement.

(b) Should the revisions to the Work make it necessary in the opinion of the Publishers substantially to re-originate production of the Work for the issue of a revised or new edition then the royalties payable on all copies sold of the first impression of such revised edition shall revert, as relevant, to the beginning of the rates of royalty as set out in Clause 12 and relevant subsections (a) (b) (e) and (f) as provided under the terms of this Agreement.

22. Remainders/Disposal of Stock
If, after a period of two years from the date of first publication, the Work shall in the opinion of the Publishers have ceased to have a remunerative sale, the Publishers shall be at liberty to dispose of any copies remaining on hand as a remainder or overstock. The Author shall be given three weeks notice of the Publishers'

intention to remainder the Work and shall have the option to purchase all or any of such stock at stated remainder price, plus freight, for disposal as the Author sees fit. If the price obtained is more than the cost of production the Publishers shall pay to the Author 10 per cent of the net amounts received by the Publisher.

23. Termination of Contract

The Author may terminate this agreement by summary notice in writing to the Publishers if the Publishers at any time by themselves or anyone acting on their behalf fail to comply with any of the Clauses or conditions set forth in this Agreement within three months after written notice from the Author to rectify such failure, or should the Publishers go into liquidation other than voluntary liquidation for the purpose of and immediately followed by reconstruction, then in either event all rights granted under this Agreement shall revert to the Author forthwith and without further notice, without prejudice to all rights of the Publishers in respect of any contracts or negotiations properly entered into by them with any third party prior to the date of such reversion, without prejudice to any claim which the Author may have for damages or otherwise and without prejudice to any monies already paid or then due to the Author from the Publishers.

24. Reprint Reversion of Rights

If the Work shall become out of print and unavailable in any English-language edition issued or licensed by the Publishers and if there is no agreement in existence between the Publishers and a third party for the publication within a reasonable period of a sub-licensed edition in the English language, then the Author may give notice in writing to the Publishers to reprint or reissue the Work within twelve months. In the event of the Publishers' failure to do so, all the Publishers' right in the Work (but not those deriving from the option in Clause 25 hereof) shall terminate upon the expiration of the said notice, without prejudice to all rights of the Publishers and any third party in respect of any agreement previously entered into by the Publishers hereunder with any such party.

Force Majeure

The Work will not be deemed out of print nor will the Publishers be liable because of delays caused by wars, civil riots, strikes, fires, lock-outs, acts of God, government restrictions or because of other circumstances beyond the Publishers' control.

25. First Option on Future Work

The Publishers shall have the first option to read and consider for publication the Author's next Work suitable for publication in volume form, and the Author shall offer to the Publishers for the purpose the same rights and territories as those covered by this Agreement. Such work shall be the subject of a fresh agreement between the Author and the Publishers, on terms which shall be fair and reasonable. If no terms have been agreed for its publication the Author shall be at liberty to enter into an agreement with another Publisher provided that the Author shall not subsequently accept from anyone else terms less favourable than are offered by the Publishers. The Publishers shall exercise this option within two months of receipt of the complete typescript or detailed outline, except that they shall not be required to exercise it until two months after the publication of the Work which is the subject of this Agreement.

26. Moral Rights

The Author hereby asserts to the Publishers and to their licensees her moral right of paternity (as originator) in the Work.

The following notice shall appear on the same page as the Copyright notice followed by the Author's name and the year of publication printed on all copies of the Work:

'The right of ***(Author's Name) to be identified as the Author of this Work has been asserted by her in accordance with the Copyright, Designs and Patents Act, 1988.'

27. Agency

The Author hereby Authorises and empowers her Agent: **

to collect and receive all sums of money payable to the Author under the terms of the Agreement and declares that ***_____ receipt shall be a good and valid discharge to all persons paying such monies to them and that they shall be empowered to act in all matters arising out of this Agreement unless the Publishers are notified in writing otherwise by the Author.

28. Arbitration

If any difference or dispute shall arise between the Author and the Publishers touching the meaning of this Agreement or the rights and liabilities of the parties thereto, the same shall be referred in the first instance to the arbitration of two persons (one to be named by each party) or their mutually agreed umpire, in accordance with the provisions of the Arbitration Acts 1950-1980 or any amending or substituted statute for the time being in force.

29. *Interpretation*
The headings in this Agreement are for convenience only and shall not affect its interpretation.

30. *Governing Law*
This Agreement shall be construed in accordance with **Irish/British law and the parties hereto submit and agree to the jurisdiction of the **Irish/British courts.

Signed: _____
Author

Witness _____

Signed _____
Publisher/Director
(Attic Press Limited)

Witness _____

Date _____

Encls **(1) Author/Book Profile form
**(2) Information on preparing your disc for Attic Press.

Sample Royalty Statement

Publisher's Name/ Address/Tel No./Fax No./VAT No.
Imprint Name: Print run:

Author/s: Royalty Statement No:
Statement Address   Title:
(Agent/Author)   Account No:

Royalty Statement: For period ended: 31/03/95   Date Issued:

Hardback	Total Sales to date	Total Sales this period	Published Price HB £15	
Home sales	200	10 @ £15 x 10% (Retail)		£15.00
	500	50 @ £15 x 10% (Wholesale)		£37.50
	700	60		£ 52.50
Export sales				
	50	00 @ £15 x 10% (Eur)		£
	50	00 @ £15 x 10% (Australia)		£
	50	00 @ £15 x 10% (New Zealand)		£
	50	00 @ £15 x 10% (USA)		£
	50	00 @ £15 x 10% (Canada)		£
	250	00		£00.00
Paperback			**Published Price PB £5**	
Home sales	1500	500 @ £5 x 7.5% (Retail)		£187.50
	2500	1000 @ £5 x 7.5% (Wholesale)		£187.50
	4000	1500		£375.00
Export sales	50	00 @ £5 x 7.5% (Eur)		£
	50	00 @ £5 x 7.5% (Australia)		£
	50	00 @ £5 x 7.5% (New Zealand)		£
	50	00 @ £5 x 7.5% (USA)		£
	50	00 @ £5 x 7.5% (Canada)		£
	250	00		£00.00
Total sales	5200	1560		

	Sales earnings during this period	£427.50
	Amount withheld from previous period	£ 50.00
Other earnings:		
	Subsidiary right (USA) details attached	£000.00
	Subsidiary right (NZ) details attached	£000.00
	Extract reprinted in *The Times* £50 @ 50%	£ 25.00
	Total Earnings:	£502.50

Deductions:		
	Advance/Amount Paid	£
	20% Withholding on Returns Royalty	£100.50
	Unearned Balance B/F	£
	Book Purchases (invoices attached)	£ 15.00
	Rechargeable Items	£
	Total Deductions	£
	Net Amount Payable	**£387.00**
	VAT @	£

Balance Unearned Carried Forward/	**£000.00**
Amount Payable 30/6/95 ~~or 30/12/95~~	**£387.00**

Appendix D
The Minimum Terms Agreement (MTA)

The Writers' Guild and the Society of Authors have been negotiating, since the mid 1970s, to try to persuade British publishers to accept a model contract known as the Minimum Terms Agreement. The title is misleading however because several of the clauses in the MTA are considerably more favourable to the author than those in the average publisher's contract. Many publishers have strongly resisted attempts to impose the MTA, with arguments around the clause which specifies a negotiable length of licence, (ie to reduce the period which includes the life of the author plus 50 year after her death clause to a fixed period). The following are the conditions which writers' organisations are pressing to have accepted.

1. Either party has the opportunity to ask for the terms of the contract to be reviewed every ten years.
2. Any income received from sub-licences are to be paid immediately, once the advance is earned.
3. The cost of indexing, if not done by the author, is to be shared equally between author and publisher.
4. The author is to receive 12 free copies of a hardback, and 20 free copies of a paperback.
5. The author is to be informed of the size of the print run.
6. There is to be full discussion prior to signing the contract about illustrations, quotations, etc, and agreement as to who will pay. Normally the publishers will pay some or all of the costs involved.
7. There is to be full consultation on all illustrations, the jacket, the blurb and the publication date.
8. The author is to be invited to make suggestions for publicity, and to be shown the proposed distribution list for review copies.
9. The author is to be consulted in full before any major sub-licences are granted.
10. The minimum royalty scale proposed in the MTA (not applicable for some specialist and heavily illustrated books) is:
For hardbacks: between 10 - 15 per cent on published price (home sales) or publisher's received price (exports and wholesale) depending on print run. On small reprint, the royalty may revert back to 10 per cent.
For paperbacks: A minimum of 7.5 per cent rising to 10 per cent after 50,000 copies on the home market and a minimum of 6 per cent of the published price. If the paperback rights are sub-

licensed, the author is to receive at least 60 per cent of income, rising to 70 per cent at a point to be agreed.

11. Minimum percentages to be paid to the author from sub-license income are:

American rights	85 per cent
Translations:	80 per cent
First serial rights	90 per cent
TV and radio dramatisations	90 per cent
Film rights	90 per cent
Anthology/Quotation rights	60 per cent
TV and radio readings	75 per cent
Merchandising	80 per cent

Appendix E

Code of Practice: Guidelines for Publishers

The following Code of Practice has been adopted by the British and Irish (Clé) Publishers' Associations. The Code, which was first issued in 1982, contains a set of recommended principles to its members in their dealings with authors. It is important to note that this Code does not apply to an agreement where an author invests money in the publication of a work, for example, vanity publishing (see section Chapter 1). This Code gives guidance only.

A constructive and cooperative relationship between the author (and agents and/or representatives acting for them) and your publisher is vital to successful publishing. There can be dissatisfaction if the book does not become the success the author and publisher hoped for but also because of misunderstandings of the publishing contract or because the 'customs of trade' are not understood or appreciated by the author.

Book publishing is so varied in its scope that contracts are likely to contain many variations between, for example, different types of book with different markets, different levels of editorial involvement by the publisher and between established and relatively new authors. Total uniformity of contract or practice is therefore impracticable. Some academic, educational and reference books and works based on a variety of contributions may be subject to special considerations, though the necessity to follow the general principles of this Code remain.

1. The publishing contract must be clear, unambiguous and comprehensive, and must be honoured in both the letter and the sprit.

Matters which particularly need to be defined in the contract include:

(i) a title which identifies the work or (for incomplete works) the nature and agreed length and scope of the work.

(ii) the nature of the rights conferred — the ownership of the copyright (an assignment or an exclusive licence) whether all-volume rights (or part of the volume rights or more than volume rights) and the territories and languages covered.

(iii) the time scale for delivery of the manuscript and for publication.

(iv) the payments, royalties and advances (if any) to be paid, what they are in respect of and when they are due.

(v) the provisions for sub-licensing.

(vi) the responsibility for preparing the supporting materials (eg indexes, illustrations, etc) in which the author holds the copyright, and for obtaining permissions and paying for the supporting materials in which the copyright is held by third parties.

(vii) the termination and reversion provisions of the contract.

Should the parties subsequently agree changes to the contract, these should be recorded in writing between them.

2. The author should retain ownership of the copyright, unless there are good reasons otherwise.

An exclusive licence should be sufficient to enable the publisher to exploit and protect most works effectively. In particular fields of publishing (eg encyclopaedic and reference works, certain types of academic works, publishers' compilations edited from many outside contributions, some translations and works particularly vulnerable to copyright infringement because of their extensive international sale) it may be appropriate for the copyright to be vested in the publisher.

3. The publisher should ensure that an author who is not professionally represented has a proper opportunity for explanation of the terms of the contract and the reasons for each provision.

4. The contract must set out reasonable and precise terms for the reversion of rights.

When a publisher has invested in the development of an author's work on the market, and the work is a contribution to the store of literature and knowledge, and the publisher expects to market the work actively for many years, it is reasonable to acquire volume rights for the full term of the copyright, on condition that there are safeguards providing for reversion in appropriate circumstances.

The circumstances under which the grant of rights acquired by the publisher will revert to the author (eg fundamental breach of contract by the publisher, or when a title has been out of print or has not been available on the market for a stipulated time) should form a part of the formal contract. In addition, a reversion of particular rights that either have never been successfully exploited by the publishers, or which are not subject to any current (or immediately anticipated) licence or edition, may, after a reasonable period from their first acquisition and after proper notice, be returned on request to the author, provided that such particular reversions do not adversely affect other retained rights (eg the absence of an English language edition should not affect the licensing publisher's interest in a translated edition still in print) and provided that payments made by the publisher to or on behalf of the author have been earned.

5. The publisher must give the author a proper opportunity to share in the success of the work.

In general, the publishing contract should seek to achieve a fair balance of reward for author and publisher. On occasion it may be appropriate, when the publisher is taking an exceptional risk in publishing a work, or the origination costs are unusually high, for the author to assist the publication of the work by accepting initially a low royalty return. In such cases, it is also appropriate for the publisher to agree that the author should share in success by, for example, agreeing the royalty rates should increase to reflect that success.

If under the contract the author receives an outright or single payment, but retains ownership of the copyright, the publisher should be prepared to share with the author any income derived from a use of the work not within the reasonable contemplation of the parties at the time of the contract.

6. The publisher must handle manuscripts promptly, and keep the author informed of progress.

All manuscripts and synopses received by the publisher, whether solicited or unsolicited, should be acknowledged as soon as received. The author may be told at that time when to expect to hear further, but in the absence of any such indications at least a progress report should be sent by the publisher to the author within six weeks of receipt. A longer time may be required in the case of certain works, eg those requiring a fully detailed assessment, particularly in the cases where the opinion of specialist readers may not be readily available, and in planned co-editions, but they should be informed of a likely date when a report may be expected.

Note: It is important for the publisher to know if the manuscript or synopsis is being simultaneously submitted to any other publisher.

7. The publisher must not cancel a contract without good and proper reason.

It is not easy to define objectively what constitutes unsuitability for publication of a commissioned manuscript or proper cause for the cancellation of a contract, since these may depend on a variety of circumstances. In any such case, however, the publisher must give the author sufficiently detailed reasons for rejection.

When the publisher requires changes in a commissioned manuscript as a condition of publication, these should be clearly set out in writing.

Note: In the case of unsolicited manuscripts or synopses, the publisher is under no obligation to give reasons for rejection, and is entitled to ask the author for return postage.

Time

If an author fails to deliver a completed manuscript according to the contract or within the contracted period, the publisher may be entitled (*inter alia*) to a refund of money advanced on account. However, it is commonly accepted that (except where time is of the essence) monies advances are not reclaimable until the publisher has given proper notice of intent to cancel the contract within a reasonable period from the date of such notice. Where the advance is not reclaimed after the period of notice has expired, it is reasonable for the publisher to retain an option to publish the work.

Standard and quality

If an author has produced the work in good faith and with proper care, in accordance with the terms of the contract, but the publisher decides not to publish on the grounds of quality, the publisher should not expect to reclaim on cancellation that part of any advance that has already been paid to the author. If, by contrast, the work has not been produced in good faith and with proper care, or the work does not conform to what has been commissioned, the publisher may be able to reclaim the advance.

Defamation and illegality

The publisher is under no obligation to publish a work that there is reason to believe is defamatory or otherwise illegal.

Change of circumstance

A change in the publisher's circumstances or policies is not a sufficient reason for declining to publish a commissioned work without compensation.

Compensation

Depending on the grounds for rejection

(i) the publisher may be liable for further advances due and an additional sum may be agreed to compensate the author, or

(ii) the author may be liable to repay the advances received.

In the former case, the agreement for compensation may include an obligation on the author to return advances and compensation paid (or part of them) if the work is subsequently placed elsewhere.

Resolution of disputes

Ideally, terms will be agreed privately between the parties, but in cases of dispute the matter should be put to a mutually agreed informal procedure, or if this cannot be agreed, to arbitration or normal legal procedures.

8. The contract must set out the anticipated timetable for publication.

The formal contract must make clear the time scale within which the author undertakes to deliver the complete manuscript, and within which the publisher undertakes to publish it. It should be recognised that in particular cases there may be valid reasons for diverging from these stated times, or for not determining strict time scales, and each party should be willing to submit detailed reasons for the agreement of the other party, if these should occur.

9. The publisher should be willing to share precautions against legal risks not arising from carelessness by the author.

For example:

Libel

While it remains the primary responsibility of the author to ensure that the work is not libellous, particularly that it cannot be arraigned as a malicious libel, the publisher may also be liable. Libel therefore demands close co-operation between authors and publishers, in particular in sharing the costs of reading for libel and of any insurance considered to be desirable by the parties.

10. The publisher should consider assisting the author by funding additional costs involved in preparing the work for publication.

If under the contract the author is liable to pay for supporting materials, for example, for permission to use other copyright material, for the making and use of illustrations and maps, for costs of indexing, etc, the publisher may be willing to fund such expenses, to an agreed ceiling, that could reasonably be recovered against any such monies as may subsequently become due to the author.

11. The publisher must ensure that the author receives a regular and clear account of sales made and money due.

The period during which sales are to be accounted for should be defined in the contract and should be followed, after a period also to be laid down in the contract, by a royalty statement and a remittance of monies due. Publishers should always observe these dates and obligations scrupulously. Accounts should be rendered at least annually, and in the first year of publication the author may reasonably expect an intermediate statement and settlement. The initial pattern of sales of some educational books, however, may make such intermediate payment impracticable.

The current model royalty statement (1979) issued by the Association of Authors' Agents, the Publishers' Association, the Society of Authors and the Writers' Guild, or the information suggested by it, should be seen as a guide, and details of the statement should be adequately explained.

The publisher should pay the author on request the appropriate share of any substantial advances received from the major sub-licensing agreements by the end of the month following the month of receipt (providing monies already advanced have been earned, and proper allowance made for returned stock; allowance may also need to be made if very substantial advances have been outstanding for an extended period of time).

The publisher should be prepared, on request, to disclose details of the number of copies printed, on condition that the author (and the agent) agree not to disclose the information to any other party.

Publishers should be prepared to give authors indications of sales to date, which must be realistic bearing in mind either unsold stock which may be returned by booksellers or stock supplied on consignment.

12. The publisher must ensure that the author can clearly ascertain how any payments due from sub-licensed agreements will be calculated.
Agreements under which the calculation of the author's share of any earnings is dependent on the publisher's allocation of direct costs and overheads can result in dissatisfaction unless the system of accounting is clearly defined.

13. The publisher should keep the author informed of important design, promotion, marketing and sub-licensing decisions.
Under the contract, final responsibility for decision on the design, promotion and marketing of a book is normally vested in the publisher. Nevertheless, the fullest reasonable consultation with the author on such matters is generally desirable, both as a courtesy and in the interests of the success of the book itself. In particular the author should, if interested and available, be consulted about the proposed jacket, jacket copy and major promotional and review activities, be informed in advance of

publication date and receive advance copies by that date. When time permits, the publisher should consult the author about the disposition of major sub-leases, and let the author have a copy of the agreement on request.

14. The integrity of the author's work should always be protected.

The author is entitled to ensure that the editorial integrity of the work is maintained. No significant alterations to the work (ie alterations other than those which could not reasonably be objected to) should be made without the author's consent, particularly where the author has retained the copyright.

The author who has retained ownership of the copyright is entitled also to be credited with the authorship of the work, and to retain the ownership of the manuscript.

15. The publisher should inform the author clearly about opportunities for amendment of the work in the course of production.

The economics of printing make the incorporation of authors' textual revisions after the book has been set extremely expensive. Publishers should always make it clear to authors, before a manuscript is put in hand, whether proofs are to be provided or not, on whom the responsibility for reading them rests and what scale of author's revisions would be acceptable to the publisher. If proofs are not being provided, the author should have the right to make final corrections to the copy-edited typescript, and the publisher should take responsibility for accurately reproducing this corrected text in type.

16. It is essential that both the publisher and the author have a clear common understanding of the significance attaching to the option clause in a publishing contract.

The option on an author's work can be of great importance to both parties. Options should be carefully negotiated, and the obligations that they impose should be clearly stated and understood on both sides. Option clauses covering more than one work may be undesirable, and should only be entered into with particular care.

17. The publisher should recognise that the remaindering of stock may effectively end the author's expectation of earnings.

Before a title is remaindered, the publisher should inform the author and offer all or part of the stock to the author on the terms expected from the remainder dealer. Whether any royalty, related to the price received in such sales, should be paid is a matter to be determined by the publisher and the author at the time of the contract.

18. The publisher should endeavour to keep the author informed of changes in the ownership of the publishing rights and of any changes in the imprint under which a work appears.

Most publishers will expect to sign their contracts on behalf of their successors and assigns, just as most authors will sign on behalf of their executors, administrators and assigns. But if changes in rights ownership or of publishing imprint subsequently occur, a publisher should certainly inform and, if at all possible, accommodate an author in these new circumstances.

19. The publisher should be willing to help the author and the author's estate in the administration of literary affairs.

For example, the publisher should agree to act as an expert witness in questions relating to the valuation of a literary estate.

20. Above all, the publisher must recognise the importance of co-operating with the author in an enterprise in which both are essential. This relationship can be fulfilled only in an atmosphere of confidence, in which authors get the fullest possible credit for their work and achievements.

Note: This Code of Practice applies only to agreements whereby an author assigns or licenses an interest in the copyright of a work to a publisher, and does not apply to agreements whereby an author invest money in the publication of a work.

(The Code of Practice is Copyright The Publishers' Association 1982)

Appendix F

An Example of House Style

All publishers have their own special house style. If you have been commissioned by a publisher, or are writing with one publisher in mind, you should obtain a copy of their house style and follow it carefully. A house style sets out detailed guidelines for typing or keying in your Ms, advice on such details as the use of capital letters, presentation of quotations, preferred spellings, punctuation, the handling of footnotes, endnotes and many other topics. If you are preparing your Ms 'on spec', the following guidelines, which Attic Press gives all its authors (and pleads with them to follow), will help you.

For further reference use the *Concise* (or shorter) *Oxford English Dictionary*, the *Oxford Dictionary for Writers and Editors* and *Harts Rules for Compositors and Editors* (OUP).

Non-sexist, racist and classist language

We in Attic Press do not publish books which are in any way damaging or offensive to women and/or people of any class, race or sexual orientation. We endorse the actions of those outside the publishing industry who are endeavouring to eradicate words, phrases and long established habits of communication which belittle, ignore or insult vast sections of society.

When referring to either or both sexes, but not specifically to the male sex, the words *man* and *men* should be avoided. Alternatives are *person, people, women* and *men*. This may seem a trivial linguistic convention, but in fact it conveys the impression that women are absent, silent, or simply less important than men. Avoiding *he, his* and *him* can be more difficult, since the repeated use of *he* or *she, his* or *her* can be clumsy and boring. But they, their, them and she can often be used instead.

Highly sex-stereotyped words can usually be replaced by alternatives, such as:

Authoress	Author
Foreman	Supervisor
Housewife	Housekeeper
Man-hour	Work-hour
Man-made	Synthetic, artificial
Mankind	People
Manpower	Workforce
Poetess	Poet

Usherette	Usher
Waitress	Waiter
Watchman	Guard

Avoid references which define women in terms of their relationships with men. Do not describe women as girls when they clearly are not. The prefix Ms is preferable to either Miss or Mrs. References to married couples should present both partners as equals for example, Sara and Michael Kelly, not 'Mr' and Mrs Michael Kelly' or 'Michael Kelly and his wife Sara'.

Spelling
Chambers Twentieth Century Dictionary, ed, William Geddie (Edinburgh 1959) is the best authority for spelling.
The use of s is preferred to the American use of z and the suffix ise, not ize, where either is permissible. However, in "compromise", 'supervise', etc the 's' is essential as it is not part of a suffix. In 'analyse' etc use -yse rather than -yze. Watch out for words with alternative spelling connection, premise, medieval, encyclopedia and judgement (but judgment in legal works) are preferred.

*Accents and cedillas*Where foreign words have been absorbed into the English language, accents can be omitted unless they affect the pronunciation, for example, *elite, role, regime* (unless italicised as in, for example, *ancient regime*). Accents are used in words like *cliché, débâcle, résumé, tête-à-tête, café and protégé*. All foreign words should be carefully checked for accuracy. Irish accents should be used throughout. These should be marked on hard copy and not coded on disc.

Apostrophes
Do not insert an apostrophe in plurals such as the 1880s, MPs but use for possessives like the MP's house, St James's Park, Guinness's and where the 's' is nearly always omitted for example, in ancient and classical names, Venus', Mars', Socrates'. No apostrophe should be put before teens, twenties, thirties or before phone, plane, cello or bus. When a noun ending in 's' is used adjectivally, the apostrophe may be omitted, for example, 'The Thirty Years War'. Do not use apostrophe for phone, flue, bus, plane.

Nouns of multitude: a company board, a committee, government, etc, are normally singular.

Headings
Do not underline or punctuate the end of headings or subheadings. Ensure all chapter and subheadings are identical with wording on contents page.

Punctuation
Use full stops sparingly. Where abbreviation is partially or wholly lower case no full stop is needed, eg Ms, Mt, St, Dr, Ltd, eds, but use commas before ie, eg and etc. Units of measurement never require a full stop. Initials require full stops E A Ashe. Omit full points after all headings and after names and addresses printed below prefaces, quotations, letters, etc. The most difficult punctuation mark to handle is the comma. This is because it has a grammatical function in dividing sub-ordinate parts of the sentence from each other and a rhetorical function in guiding the pauses of the reader. The rules for one often contradict those for the other. The only safe and simple rule is that it is better to underpunctuate than overpunctuate.

The colon is used: to introduce lists, to introduce sentences enlarging upon an initial broad statement, and to introduce formal or exact quotation.

The semi-colon, half-way between the comma and the full stop, is used: to separate two sentences connected in sense but not joined by and, but, or to separate items in a list where the comma is used inside the items of the list.

Hyphenation
Use sparingly but consistently do not, for example, go from *hill side*, through *hill-side*, to *hillside*. Hyphens can be used to aid meaning or if the text is ambiguous without it for example 're-count' has a different meaning from 'recount'. Never divide a word, which can be spelt without a hyphen, at the end of a line, either on hard copy or on disc.

Do not hyphenate *no one, cooperate, coordinate, childbirth*. Hyphenate *dining-room, working-class, ten-year-old, out-of-date, five-year-plan*. Use in compound adjectives which precede nouns. No hyphen is necessary, however, if part of the compound adjective consists of a numeral. For example, a 5ft 11in woman a six mile journey. The number and the measurement is abbreviated They are spaced as separate words when the measurement is written out in full. Compound nouns which are sufficiently familiar as one word are preferred unless awkward spelling results. If in doubt omit hyphens altogether or consult *Harts Rules*.

Ellipses/points of omission
Use three points (...) to indicate an omission from a quotation. Do not use ellipses at beginning or end of quotation, as it is obvious that it is only an extract.

Parentheses (round) and square brackets
Use parentheses as brackets in, for example, *She looked pale (she had been ill)*. Also use parentheses at the end of displayed indented quotes if a reference is needed. Do not put a full point after the reference. Square brackets are used within quotations to indicate that author's additions are not found in the original.

Solidus/oblique stroke (/)
Where used in, for example, the fiscal year 1993/4, mark clearly.

Dashes (hypen, en-rules, em-rules)
Hyphen's (-) are used for word breaks. En-rule's (- not found in some software packages!) are used for dates, for example, 1955-6, the 1914-18 war, pp. 120-21. Em-rules (longer than hyphen and En-rule) are used for text breaks. See **Glossary**.

Italics
When italics are to be used omit any quotations marks. Use for foreign words which have not entered into common use, also for titles of books, journals and magazines, as well as titles of plays, works of art, ships, films. If you are presenting your text on a floppy disc, underline the words or mark them with a highlighter on the hardcopy to indicate italics. Do not italicise text on disc.

Capitals
These should be used as sparingly as possible and not for emphasis. When you use capitals to make a distinction between, for example, labour and Labour, be consistent throughout text.

Titles
It is not necessary to use a capital when these are mentioned, for example, the bishop, the prime minister/taoiseach, president, unless making a point.

Religious and other institutions
It is not necessary to use a capital when a title is mentioned unless

you are making a particular point, for example, 'the Catholic Church's obsession with censorship...' otherwise the catholic church, the bishop, buddhism, zionism, the state, the press, etc.

Periods of history
Iron Age, Celtic Age, Middle Ages, the Renaissance, The First World War (not World War 1) but two world wars.

Geographical
Use lower case for regional areas, such as northern England, western France, but capital when referring to a political entity, for example, Northern Ireland.

Political
Use initial capitals when referring to a specific political party or grouping, eg Labour. Use lower case for the left of the party, right-wing politics, or the women's movement.

Abbreviations
Use BBC, RTE, USA, EC, TUC, ICTU, UN without full stops. MPs, TDs, NGOs require no apostrophe. Where an abbreviation is partially or wholly lower case, no full stop is needed if the final letter of the word is used in the abbreviation eg Ms, Ltd, eds or St for Saint. Use 'for example' and 'that is' rather than eg and ie.
Ampersand (&) should be used only in names of companies and occasionally in facsimile quotations from early documents. For scripture references use arabic numerals, dividing chapter and verse by colon: eg Genesis 2:14 Psalms 18:47 2 Corinthians 4:8. For drama references. Act 111, scene ii, line 297, to appear as 111.ii.297.

Dates
Dates given in full should be written as 8 March 1994, without punctuation, and not 8th March, 1994 or March 8, 1994. When the year is not given, the form should be the same, ie 8 March. Write 'the 1970s' (not the 1970's), 'the thirties' (not the 30s). BC should follow the date and AD should precede it. Periods for BC have to be spelt out in full (for example, 330-325BC). Except in chapter or section headings, dates AD are best abbreviated, for instance, to 1993-6 or (for a financial or academic year) 1993/4. Underline c. (for Circa) to show italic and type the date close up to the full stop.

Figures/numbers
Generally spell out all numbers from one to ten (in more technical books) or under 100 (in more literary books) and always spell out

numbers at the beginning of a new sentence. Also spell round numbers and approximate numbers like 'five hundred' or 'three hundred and fifty thousand'. Percentages should always be in figures, for example, 5.5 per cent. Write 'per cent' in the text '%' in tables or in notes which cite a number of statistics. The fewest possible figures should be given 68-9, 125-6, 1,500-1,600, *but* 90-91, 100-103, 216-18, 1,255-66. Adopt a consistent rule of treatment of thousands: either 5400 but 54000 or 5,400 and 54,000. In tables, the rule may have to be broken to make sure that four and five-digit numbers line up.

Quotation Marks
Single quotes take precedence over double. Single quotes are used for all dialogue, quoted words or (short) passages while double quotation marks are used for dialogue or quotes within a quote. Single quotation marks are used for articles, parts of a book, poems and song. Quotations over 320 words long should be indented with a line space above and below. Do not indent first line of extract but do indent second, third paragraph, etc, where necessary by marking hard copy.

Quotations
Excessive quotations from other works should be avoided (see copyright permissions). In certain cases, however, it will be essential to quote extensively from a particular source.

The original spelling of quotations should normally be followed exactly. In some books, however, there may be a case for modernising spelling or silently correcting eccentricities. Spelling (or other) errors found in the original are usually retained in quotations and followed by (sic). To determine whether the first letter of a quotation should be a capital or not, you should consistently either follow the original, or standardise according to the way in which the quotation fits your text.

Where words have been omitted from a quoted passage, use ellipses distinguish consistently between an unfinished sentence (three dots) and a completed sentence (a full stop followed by three dots, ie, four dots in all. Any insertions of your own should be enclosed in square brackets. State 'my italics' where appropriate. Do please quote from the same edition of a book throughout your typescript unless there is a special reason not to do so.

Punctuation that is part of the quoted matter is usually placed inside quotes. When a complete sentence is quoted, the full point goes inside the quotes but when only the last part of a sentence is quoted it is better to place the full point outside the quotes.

We use the following rules to punctuate short quotations which run on in the text. Where a word of phrase (even a very long phrase) is quoted, the closing quotation marks precedes the full stop. Where a sentence is quoted (that is, anything with a subject and main verb, whether or not it forms a complete sentence in the original), the full stop precedes the closing quotation mark. Other marks (colon, semi-colon, etc) should be placed according to sense.

The punctuation of dialogue usually goes inside the quotation marks. Even broken dialogue normally follows the pattern of speech pauses so that the comma after the first phrase goes inside the quotes. For example: 'The traffic is light,' she said, 'so I'll be on time.'

Quotations displayed as extracts

Longer quotations (more than 60 words) should be broken off from the text and set out as 'extracts'. Occasionally shorter passages may be worth treating as extracts, so that they can either be compared with longer passages, or for emphasis, very short extracts can look strange in print. When typing or keying in extracts, indent them and use double-spacing with an extra space above and below. There is no need to indent the first line of the extract further, even if it begins a new paragraph in the original. Do not use quotation marks, except where they are needed to indicate dialogue within the extract itself.

Sources

If your references are given in notes (see below), place the note indicator after the quotation, whether it is set out as an extract or run on in the text.

If you are using the author-date system (see below), it is often neater to incorporate the reference into the sentence before the extract. Where the reference follows the extract it should be in parentheses, following the final full stop of the extract, but without a full stop of its own. Where a shorter quotation is run on in the text the reference in parentheses is best typed before the full stop, thus: '... in space' (Campbell, 1994, p. 70).

Notes and References

The style and form these should take depends very much on the book and the audience it is being aimed at, so in every case this should be discussed with the editor in advance of the final draft being typed or keyed in.

Substantive, as opposed to reference, notes should be avoided as far as possible. The placing of notes (whether as true footnotes, or at the end of the chapter or book) depends largely on the market (academic or non-academic) and costing of the book (extra pages are needed to set out notes separately). Discuss this with your editor as early as possible.

Whether your notes are to be set as footnotes or as endnotes, they should not be typed at the foot of the page, but at the end of the chapter or at the end of the typescript.

Number the notes consecutively through each chapter. It is important that no notes be called, for example, 15a. If you need to add a note during revision, please renumber the rest of the notes in the chapter.

Note indicators in the text should be placed at a natural break in the sentence and should follow any punctuation except a dash. Type the indicator above the line, without parentheses.

Avoid attaching note indicators to chapter headings or sub-headings as they look odd.

Do not attach ordinary chapter notes to table headings or figure captions as it may not be possible to place the tables and figures precisely enough to maintain the numbering sequence. Instead, notes and an indication of source should go under a table. General explanatory notes about a figure and an indication of the source should be incorporated in the caption. Tables and figures should be numbered consecutively by chapter, ie Figure 1.1, 1.2, Table 1.1, 1.2 etc.

Bibliographies and References
A bibliography should be arranged in alphabetical sequence by author's name (second name first in capitals). It should include date and place of publication as well as the publisher, for example.

> REYNOLDS, Lorna *Tasty Food for Hasty Folk*, Dublin: Attic Press, 1992.

Where there is more than one reference under a particular author's name, the references should be consistently ordered either chronologically or alphabetically by title. The form of bibliographical citation and the reference system you choose will normally be dictated by current usage in your own discipline.

Where references appear in the notes and do not interrupt the flow of the text a system may be used with or without a full bibliography at the end of the book. Where there is no bibliography, a full reference is given the first time a work is mentioned in a chapter, for example Daly, Mary *Women and Poverty* (Attic Press, Dublin, 1992) pp 112-115.

For articles in edited volumes, use: Barry, Ursula. Movement, Change and Reaction: The struggle over reproductive rights in Ireland in *The Abortion papers*, ed. Ailbhe Smyth (Attic, Dublin, 1992) pp 107-118

After the first reference in the chapter, further references consist of the author's second name and the title, or, if it is long, a short version of the title: Barry, *The Abortion Papers*, p 107

If you prefer, shortened references to articles can use the journal title, or the editor's name, instead of the article title, provided this is done consistently, eg Barry, in Smyth (ed) p. xx

It is preferable to use a short title rather than *op. cit.* which is less readily recognisable and can be ambiguous. However, where reference is made to the same work as that given in the immediately preceding note, it is acceptable to write: *ibid.* p. 25.

Author-date

Sometimes the name of author and the date is given as a reference within the text. This is the most common reference system used in the sciences. It largely eliminates the need for notes. The disadvantage is that the reader has to turn to the reference list at the end of the book to trace the source, since a date is generally less informative than a short title. The reference in parentheses in the text gives the author's second name and the date of publication. If two or more works by the author have the same date, distinguish them by using, a, b, etc. Use the following form consistently: (Barry, 1992a, p 107--)

Where the author's name is mentioned in the body of the sentence, the reference in parentheses simply consists of the date and, if necessary, the page. For a repeated reference, do not use *ibid*, but simply repeat the date. If both author and date are clear from the context, a page reference alone, in parentheses, is enough, but use the form (p. 60), not just (60).

Where two or more references are given together, follow consistently either alphabetical order, or chronological order, or order of importance.

The date given in references in the text should be the date of the edition used. It is sometimes helpful, however, to mention the date of the original edition, or the date of the original of a translation, among the bibliographical details in the reference list.

Appendix G
Keying in your text on a word-processor

Various guides are available but technology is advancing so fast in this area that it is really more sensible to consult your publisher about:

(a) the make and model (type) of computer (hardware) you are using (eg PC/IBM, Apple, Amstrad, ICL, or other)

(b) the name and version of the operation system (eg MS Dos or Apple)

(c) the name, version and manufacture of the software you are using (eg Wordperfect, Wordstar, Word5).

(d) sizes and types of discs (3.5" and 5.25")

Don't be alarmed and don't hesitate to ask your publisher to give you clarification and guidance. If your system is not compatible with the system used by your publisher, it is likely that your word-processing programme will be able to output the text in ASCII files (check your manual) which will make your discs accessible. ASCII means that only the regular text, spacing and line breaks are saved and the text is stripped of all hidden codes thereby making it more accessible to other software packages and computer systems. As a safeguard, it is a good idea to send in both an ASCII file and non-ASCII files on your disc.

Of course, you can avoid complications by sending your publisher, preferably before you start keying in, a sample chapter (file) of your text.

It is essential that the discs are identical to the hard copy (print-out) you send, otherwise there may be time-wasting confusion. You should always include a separate sheet listing your disc files. If possible, make a new file for each chapter.

When keying in your text, keep the following points in mind. Many people use their computers like a typewriter and this can cause major (sometimes even impossible) problems for converting your disc as well as for editing, the main point to remember is to be consistent:

• Do not indent, centre, emphasise with bold type or italicise your text unless your programme is fully (100 per cent) compatible with that of the publisher - mark these instructions, with a coloured highlighter, on your hardcopy.

• All text (including all quotes, notes and bibliographies) should be double spaced.

• Key-in all text without using the return (or 'enter') key at the end of line as you would on a typewriter, just let the text flow. All word-processing packages use what is called a 'word wrap' system. This means that the length of every line is pre-set and only so many words will fit on a line. The rest will automatically fall on to the next line. The carriage return key should only be used at the end of a paragraph, never at the end of a line within a paragraph.

• Use same length of line on each page and the same number of lines per page.

• Do not 'justify' the text, as in this book. See **Glossary**

• Opening and closing quotation marks are different for most typefaces so you need to distinguish between them. One way of doing this is to use " for opening a quotation and ' for closing. For quotes within quotes use "" and ".

• Use only one space between words and following all punctuation marks. Use space bar for all spacing never use tab keys.

• Do not use automatic hyphenation at the ends of lines.

• Do not indent new paragraphs. Leave an extra line space between paragraphs.

• Be consistent in the way in which you use spacing or indentation to distinguish material such as extracts and lists from the main text.

• If you need to use characters/letters/symbols (ie á, í, ú) that are not available on your keyboard or printer, mark the hard copy clearly with a coloured pen or highlighter.

• In general do ensure that all characters are clearly distinguished.

• Use the correct lower-case characters, ie number 1 for numbers and the letter 'l' in text, the letter o and not the number 0.

• Be consistent in the way you represent a parenthetical dash. It is best to use a hyphen with a space before and after it.

• Tables and figures should be included on the disc at the end of the text. Give each a letter or code and mark in the text (giving letter or code) where they should be placed.

• Do not key in footnotes with the text under any circumstances, just give footnote number. Footnotes should be keyed in together at the end of each chapter.

• Number each page in sequence throughout (never chapter by chapter).

• Never use correcting fluid on the hard copy. Any last minute corrections should be written on to the hard copy by hand always with a colourful mark in the margin to draw attention to it.

• If your machine has recorded the total character count (both letters and spaces) or the number of words, do include this information.

• Please remember to change your printer ribbon before running out final copy for your publisher. Spare a thought for your editor's eyes as the print must be dark enough to copy, and dark enough to read!

• Print/type using one side (never two) of A4 paper.

• Start each chapter on a new page.

• Allow margins of at least one (1") inch on the left and right of page.

• Allow margins of at least two (2") inches on top and bottom of page.

• Send two identical and complete hard copies of your final text to the publisher, or one disc with identical hard copy. Remember always to keep a copy for yourself for reference, safe keeping and as insurance against loss.

• All changes will most likely take place on the hard copy which will be returned to you unless there is need for extensive revision. The changes agreed will be inserted at final production stage.

Appendix H

Proof-Readers' Correction Symbols/Marks

Corrections and alterations can be mortifying, irritating and expensive as well as causing delays. The author is expected to bear the cost of making extensive corrections to proofs (other than those attributable to publisher or printer) and is charged if authors corrections exceed a specified percentage (usually 10%) of the cost of typesetting. The author must return proofs with a specified period usually within 7 or 14 days.

Instruction	Text Mark	Margin Mark
• substitute	The dog jumped over the lady cat	z/
• transpose	The dog jumped over the cat lazy	∽
• delete	The dogs jumped over the lazy cat	ꝯ
• insert	The dog jumpd over the lazy cat	ʎe
• close up	The dog jump ed over the lazy cat	◡
• insert space	The dogjumped over the lazy cat	⼃#
• change to italic	The dog jumped over the lazy <u>cat</u>	*ital*
• change italic to upright (roman) type	The dog jumped over the lazy *cat*	*Roman*
• change to bold	The dog jumped over the lazy <u>cat</u>	*bold*
• change capital to lower case	the Ⓓog jumped over the lazy cat	*l.c.*
• change lower case to capital	The dog jumped over the lazy <u>cat</u>	*Cap*
• start a new paragraph	⌈The dog jumped over the lazy cat	*Par*
• run on	The dog jumped⌐ over the lazy cat	*run on*
• insert space between lines	The dog jumped over the lazy cat ⧣	⧣

145

Instruction	Text Mark	Margin Mark
• close up space between lines	The dog jumped ( ) over the lazy cat	*Close up*
• substitute or insert note indicator or superior	The dog jumped over the lazy cat⟨	⟨ 1 ⌄
• substitute or insert inferior	The dog jumped over the lazy cat⟨	⟨ ⌄ 2
• stet (if you make a mistake and want to restore the original	The dog jumped ~~over~~ the lazy cat	*stet*
• Move left	⌐ The dog jumped over the lazy cat	⌐
• Move right	The dog jumped over the lazy cat ⌐	⌐
• Indent	⌐The dog jumped over the lazy cat	⌐
• Cancel indent	←The dog jumped over the lazy cat	←

Appendix I

Glossary of Common Publishing Terms

Abstract: A short résumé of an article or chapter which sums up the main points. Very common in academic and STM (scientific, technical and medical) publishing.

ACE: See **ASCII**

Acetate: Transparent film

Acknowledgements: List of sources, permissions and people the author wants to thank or particularly acknowledge. Usually in preliminary pages.

Addendum: Late addition to book after printing, usually as pasted-in slip. To be avoided at all costs!

Advance: Money paid by publisher to an author/editor in advance of the publication of her book, and on account of her expected earnings (ie royalties and, usually, income from sub-licences. The amount can vary very considerably. Not all publishing houses offer an advance. The advance is related to the expected earnings of the book. The author's royalties on the book sales are then set against her advance.

AIs (Advance Information Sheets): Single sheet (A4) giving brief advance details of a forthcoming book and author profile for the trade.

Agreement (Contract): The document signed by the author and publisher which sets out the terms and conditions under which the book will be published

ALCS: The Authors' Licensing and Collecting Agency

Align: To line up type.

Ampersand: The sign '&' meaning 'and'.

Annotate: To supply additional comments to text of book.

Appendix: Additions to a book following the main text.

Arabic : figures The numerals 1,2,3,4, etc, as distinct from Roman I,II,III,IV.

Artpaper: Paper coated with china clay and polished to a high shiny finish.

Artwork: Final copy of typesetting and illustrations on camera ready copy (CRC) which is suitable for film reproduction.

Ascender: The part of a letter, such as d and h, which extends above the height of the letter x. See **Descender**.

ASCII: (American Standard Code for Information Exchange): Pronounced ASK-ee. The name of the coding scheme used by most word-processors, IBM-PCs and compatibles. ASCII files contain only regular alphabetical words and spaces and are stripped of all codes. Such (text-only) files can then be transferred between two computers without the need for translation or de-coding. Hence the request to 'save your files in ASCII format'. See **WP Format**.

Assignment: The arrangement by which one of the parties to an agreement passes to a third party the benefit of that agreement.

Asterisk: The sign *.

b/w: Abbreviation for black and white.

Backlist: Once a book is published it becomes part of the backlist, and continues to sell, as part of the publisher's 'older' books that are still in print. The backlist is the publisher's backbone as a press cannot exist on the sale of new books alone. Publishers continually look for books which will sell over a period of years — ie potential backlist titles. See **Frontlist**.

Back-up: Duplicating your files and data, usually on disc, for security purposes. Should be done regularly.

Backslash: A 45 degree downward slash '\' **See Solidus**.

Bad break: Undesirable end-of-line hyphenation of a word.

Bank paper: (copypaper) Lightweight paper from 45gsm upwards. See **Bond paper**.

Barcode: Box with lines and ISBN, on back cover of book, gives each book its own unique product code. It is presented in standardised machine-readable format and is used for sale and stock control purposes.

Biblio page: See **Copyright**

Bibliography: List of books and articles relating to written work. Usually given at end of book. Details include author, title, publisher, etc.

Binding: Forms the spine of a book. It is the process used to bond printed sheets together to secure them in a cover. Can be perfect bound (glued like most paperbacks) saddle stitched (stapled) or thread sewn (sections sewn together then glued — usually for hardbacks).

Bleed: To extend a printed image or illustration (3 mm) beyond the trimmed size of the sheet or page to allow variations in trimming.

Blurb: Short description of book, usually printed on back cover of a paperback or inside jacket of hardbound book and/or in publisher's catalogue. This is the advertising copy or sales message. Its purpose is to give some indication of what the book is about, and to intrigue, tease and tempt the potential reader to purchase your book. The best blurbs are short and pithy.

Bold or bold face: Heavier version of a typeface as distinct from light or medium.

Bond Paper: From 60 to 100gsm in weight. See **Bank**

Book Club: A subscription club for book buyers which offers selected titles at attractive discount rates compared to normal retail price.

Bottom line: Financial jargon referring to the basic figure, at foot of balance sheet, indicating net profit or loss.

Brackets: See **Parenthesis** and **Square Brackets**.

Break even: The point at which sufficient copies of a book have to be sold in order to recover the original costs of production, promotion and advances paid.

Bromide: Light sensitive paper used in photographic reproduction or phototypesetting, producing a positive image. Word is also used more liberally to mean final image.

Bug: Computer term for a defect interfering with computer operation. See **Virus**.

Bulk: Term used to describe thickness of paper in relation to book.

Bullet: A large dot used for ornamentation in text.

Byte: The smallest unit of storage in computer memory. See **Megabyte**.

Calligraphy: The art of handwriting or script drawing.

Camera Ready Copy (CRC): the final text (typed matter), with artwork, error free and in final page format in position and ready for photographing by printer.

Caption: Text accompanying and describing an illustration.

Case or Cased edition: The binding of a book with a hard cover, as opposed to paperback or limp cover.

Cast off: A word count calculated with care, to estimate the total number of characters in a text, to determine the final number of printed pages. If you are using a computer to key-in your text, check if there is an automatic word-count with the software package.

Catalogue: Publisher's list of books with a description.

CD: Compact Disc.

Character: An individual letter, space, symbol or punctuation mark. A character count is used in casting off.

Cheap editions: This term usually refers to hardcover copies of a book sold at a price below the original published price.

CIP Data: (Cataloguing in Publication). This cataloguing information appears in the preliminary pages of book. It is used by a central national archiving body for cataloguing information on all forthcoming publications. The British Library is used in both Britain and Ireland, while in the USA it is the Library of Congress.

Circa: Used before approximate dates or figures c.

CLA: (The) Copyright Licensing Agency

Closed markets: Areas, countries, regions created when local selling rights are sold to a particular agent. Booksellers in closed market areas must obtain copies of a book from the local agent rather than direct from original publisher.

Cloth: An old-fashioned term for hardcover or cased edition of book.

Co-edition: A book produced simultaneously with two or more publishers, or a packager, in different parts of the world, or in different languages, in order to reduce printing costs.

Coated paper: Art paper, for example, which has received a coating on one or both sides and has a 'glossy' appearance.

Collate: Loosely used to mean 'gather'.

Colophon: A publisher's identifying symbol. See **Logotype**.

Column: **Vertical** area of print comprising lines of the same measure.

Colour separations: The process of separating a full colour cover into the four basic printing process colours. The separated film is then used to make printing plates. See **Four Colour Process**.

Compatibility: The ability of two pieces of hardware to work in conjunction with each other.

Complimentary copy: Copy of book given free usually to media and author.

Conflicting Work: A later book by the author which might be considered to be so similar in content to the book which is the subject of the agreement that it might damage its sales.

Contract: see **Agreement**

Copy: Raw material such as Manuscript (Ms), typescript (Ts), photographs, rough drawings, etc.

Copy date: Scheduled date for delivering **Ms** to publisher or **CRC** to printer.

Copy-edited: A Ms which has been prepared for production by a copy-editor, employed by the publisher to correct such matters as punctuation, spelling, check facts, and on occasion to rewrite careless, illiterate and inaccurate work.

Copyright: The exclusive right owned by the creator of the work (author). There are two exceptions however: if an employee produces work in the course of her employment it then belongs to her employer, or if an author sells her copyright. Copyright usually expires fifty years after the end of the calendar year in which the author dies. When an Author signs a contract with a publisher she grants a licence to the publisher to exploit the copyright, while retaining overall ownership. See section on **Copyright**.

Copyright deposit: The British, Irish, Scottish and Welsh libraries are entitled, by law, to receive a number of free copies of every book published in the UK and Ireland. *(see Chapter 7 on Copyright)*

Copyright Licensing Agency: The organisation which licenses the unlawful photocopying of copyright material, passing the collected shared income to the authors and publishers concerned.

Copyright notice: The notice printed in a book, newspaper or magazine, which attributes the ownership of the copyright to the holder.

Copyright page: The title page of a book containing bibliographic information, also known as biblio page.

Counterpack: Point-of-sale box holding a small number of books.

Cover: See **Jacket**.

CRC: See **Camera Ready Copy**.

Cromalin: A plastic-proofing system for proofing four-colour artwork taken prior to printing to ensure colours are correct.

Crop: To cut back part of an illustration to give better effect or achieve better fit indicated with crop marks.

CV: (Curriculum Vitae): A short résumé of your educational and career background.

Dash: Punctuation mark used to indicate an interruption. See **En rule** and **Em rule**

Database publishing: Publishing from information stored on a computer database. Can be a fast method of producing complex material; that does not need to be re-keyed by typesetters.

Dedication: Inscription by the author dedicating book to a specific person or persons; this is included with the prelim pages.

Delivery date: The date specified in the agreement by which the Ms is to be delivered by the author to the publisher.

Descender: The part of a letter, such as g and y, which extends below the baseline or foot of the letter x. See **Ascender**.

Diphthong: Letters placed together as in æ Æ.

Direct costs: Costs attributable to a specific project, as opposed to general overheads or indirect costs; for example, the printing bill for producing a particular book is a direct cost.

Direct mailing: Advertising material sent through the post or by other means of direct delivery.

Ditto: An instruction to duplicate in order to avoid repetition and is indicated by a pair of ditto marks (" ") placed under the word or words that would otherwise be repeated.

DOS: (Disc Operating System) The operating system which controls the routines handled by computer.

Dot matrix (Printer): Pattern of dots used to create images on screen or printer.

DTP (Desk Top Publishing): The production of fully made-up pages. You need a personal computer used for word-processing, which is powerful and fast enough to take a software programme such as Pagemaker or Ventura or indeed by modifying, for example, Wordperfect or Word5 (This book has been produced with Word5) and a laser printer. You will also need specialist advice and initial capital of at least £1,500 - £2,000.

Dues: See **Subscriptions.**

Dummy: Preliminary drawing or lay-out (mock-up) of a book to give publisher feel of what final book will look like with regard to paper, size, width of spine, etc.

Dumpbins: Point-of-sale floor unit displaying large quantities of books. Paid for by publishers for use by bookshops.

Edit: To check, arrange and correct data or material before final presentation.

Edition: One or more printings (or impressions) of the same version of a book in the same kind of binding. The term 'new (or second) edition' should not be used unless the text contains major changes. Issues with only minor corrections are called reprints or impressions.

Ellipsis: Omission, indicated by three dots or points ... .

Em: Unit of measurement, based on width of the letter 'm' in printing. Its size can vary with the size of type. The term is frequently taken to mean a standard 12pt 'm', equalling roughly 1/6". There are 6 ems to an inch. Used in the same sense as parenthesis, or to indicate an interruption. See **Point.**

Embargo: Date before which information or book may not be released; often used on press releases. Sometimes ignored by the media to secure a competitive advantage!

En: Half the width of an em.

En rule: A horizontal rule or dash used to separate dates, numbers etc. It is half the width of an Em-rule.

Endmatter: The material that follows the text proper, for example, appendices, notes, bibliography and index.

Endnotes: Notes which follow the appendix or text (or relevant chapter) rather than appearing at the foot of the relevant page of text.

Endpaper: The four pages at beginning and end of a hardback book by means of which the case (cover) is attached.

Epigraph: A quotation in the preliminary pages or at the beginning of a part of chapter.

Epilogue: Closing section at the end of a novel or play.

EPOS: Electronic point of sale. Machine-readable code that can be read by a terminal at a shop check-out to establish price and used to record and reorder stock.

Erratum (errata) slip: Paper inserted in a book containing list of post-press corrections. To be avoided!

Estimate: An estimate of the cost of producing a book; an estimate of length is called a **cast-off**.

Export Market: In Ireland is refers to all countries (excluding Northern Ireland) outside Ireland. To most British it means 'all territories outside the United Kingdom of Great Britain and Northern Ireland and the Irish Republic!'

Extent: Length of a book in pages or in words.

Facsimile: An exact copy or reproduction.

FAX: Abbreviation of facsimile. Machine used to transmit copy.

Firm sale: Order placed by a bookseller from which the publishers expect no returns. In practice most publishers are flexible enough to allow at least a credit for unsold titles, to ensure goodwill and the stocking of their titles in the future.

First refusal: Another term for Option.

First serial rights: The rights which cover the sale of material to a magazine or newspaper for publication prior to publication in book form. See **Serial rights.**

Flap: The part of the jacket (cover) which is folded inside the cover of the book — 'front flap' and 'back flap'.

Floppy disc: Small plastic disc used for storing computer information. Standard sizes 5.2" or 3.5".

Flyers: Full colour copies of cover of book printed on cheaper paper and used for publicity purposes to notify trade and media of forthcoming title.

Folios: This word has a number of definitions, in printing and publishing it is normally used to mean the page number.

Font: A complete alphabet of any one typeface in a given point size.

Foreign rights: Another term for **Translation Rights.**

Footnotes: Notes explanatory to the main text, set in smaller type at the bottom of the page. See **Endnotes.**

Foreign rights: Rights to a book sold to another publisher usually to translate and issue the work in another language. See **Subsidiary Rights.**

Foreword: Introductory remarks about a book or its author, not written by the author. As distinct from Preface.

Format: Physical size and shape of book. In Britain it is expressed as height x width, in the USA and most of Europe as width x height.

Forward slash: A 45 degree rising slash '/'. Also known as a solidus or oblique.

Four colour process: Colour printing with the three primary colours (yellow, magenta, cyan) plus black. The colours are separated photographically or by scanning.

Free copies: Copies of a book sent out for review, publicity purposes and the author's complimentary copies.

Front list: Publisher's list of current and new titles See **Backlist**.

Frontmatter: See **Prelims**.

Full colour: see **Four colour process**.

Full point: Full stop.

Galley proof: Set of proofs, in long strips (fast going out of date with DTP) before page proof stage (this is now becoming the first and only stage).

Genre: A style or type of writing, for example, fiction, poetry, drama. Also used for particular kinds of fiction, for example, science fiction or romance.

Glossary: Alphabetically arranged list of terms and their meanings.

Grid: Spaced vertical and horizontal lines printed on paper or board and used for CRC layout and paste-up. Now virtually redundant with DTP.

Gross profit: In book publishing terms, the difference between the sales revenue of a book and the direct costs incurred in obtaining those sales, ie net revenue less production, promotion and royalties (advance). Contrast net profit.

gsm (or g/m2): Grams per square metre, the measure by which paper is sold and often used to describe weight of paper.

Half title: Sometimes a shortened version of the title of a book, with or without the author's name, is printed on the first right-hand page in the book, the title page — usually a design decision.

Half-tone: An image made up of dots of varying size to give the illusion of 'continuous tone'.

Hache: The symbol # to mean create space used as a proofreading mark.

Hardback/Hardcover: The book is bound in boards with imitation cloth, and equipped with a jacket.

Hard copy: Copy of text which is written, typed or printed as opposed to copy of text on disc or other retrieval system (which is soft copy).

Hardware: Computer term for computer equipment and peripherals as opposed to software programme.

Headline (running heads): The heading set at the top of each page except over chapter opening, in most non-fiction books and some novels.

Hertz: Processing speed (MHz) most micros are rates between 5Mhz up to 20 Mhz.

Home Market: See **Export Market**

House style: The publishing house editorial rules governing style, language, grammar, punctuation and appearance of type.

Hyphen: Half the length of an em-rule and thicker.

Hyphenation: Division of words.

Hype: Expression denoting promotional gimmick or campaign. Often used to mean inflated advertising.

ibid (ibidem): Abbreviated Latin 'ibidem', meaning 'in the same place': used in reference books or citations to refer to the same article, etc, as previously mentioned.

IBM compatible: A term applied to personal computers (PCs) which the manufactures claim will accept hardware and software designed to run on an IBM PC clone.

Icon: A pictorial representation of an object or function in a computer display.

idem (id): Means 'the same', used to mean the same author as before.

Imposition: The way in which the pages of a book are ordered for printing purposes so that when the paper is folded the pages will appear in the correct order.

Impression: The number of copies of a book printed at any one time without changing the printing plates. Several impressions may go into the making of a single edition.

Imprint: The name of the publisher which appears on the title page of a book, or at the foot of an advertisement. A publishing house may have several imprints.

Imprint page: See **Technical page**.

In-house: Jobs that are carried out by the staff and using the resources within the press.

In print: A term applied to a book which is currently available from the publishers, as opposed to those which have sold out and will not be reprinted which are designated as 'out of print'. The phrase 'in print' is also used to indicate the number of copies printed of a book since it was first published, eg 'there are 15,000 copies of this book in print, made up of three impressions', or 'ten of this author's books, totalling over 20,000 copies of her works in print, are in paperback editions.'

Indent: To leave space at the beginning of a line or paragraph.

Index: Alphabetical list of subjects contained in the text of a work, together with their page numbers.

Indicator: A footnote indicator is the number or symbol in the text which indicates that there is a footnote to the word or sentence.

Insert: Paper or card inserted loose in a book which is not secured in any way.

Inset: A small group of pages (often half-tones) inserted in the middle section of a book.

Inspection copy: Copy of a book (usually an educational text) supplied for examination in the hope that it will be recommended on a reading list. Books supplied 'On approval' must either be returned or paid for.

Introduction: Introduction to the subject matter of a book as distinct from Preface, Foreword.

ISBN: The initials stand for International Standard Book Number. A unique 10 digit numbering system, used world wide to identify the book title, its language, publisher.

ISSN: International Standard Serial Number - used for magazines.

Italic: Letters that slope forward.

Jacket: also called 'dust jacket', 'dust cover', the loose paper wrapper which is placed around a hardback.

Justified type: Type set so that both the left and right hand margins are aligned vertically - as in newspaper columns and this book.

Keyboard: The rows of keys on a typewriter, typesetting machine or computer.

Kilobyte (Kb): 64k = 95,000 words, 1 Mb = 150,000 words.

Lamination/varnishing: Thin transparent plastic film, available in matt or gloss, applied to the surface of book cover. Varnishing has a similar effect and is less expensive but gives less protection than lamination.

Landscape: Horizontal oblong format, ie wider than it is high (as opposed to portrait).

Layout: The arrangement of text and images on a page.

l.c.: Lower case as opposed to U/L (Upper and lower case) or caps for capitals.

Leading: White space or distance between lines of type.

Leaf: Two pages which back on to one another, or single sheet comprising two pages.

Letraset: Proprietary name of system of dry transfer characters, letters or illustrations used in preparing artwork.

Letterpress: The process of printing from a raised surface.

Licence period: The length of time for which a publisher, or her sub-licensee, may exercise the rights granted under the agreement.

Ligature: Two or more letters joined together on one body. Contrast diphthong.

Limp: The opposite to hardback where boards are used for cover. Paperbacks have a limp binding.

Line drawing: A drawing which consists of black lines, shading and solid areas, but no greys.

Liquidation: When a company collapses, usually into bankruptcy and ceases to trade.

List: All the books/titles a publisher has available for sale. See **Catalogue.**

List price: See **Published Price.**

Literal: More commonly called a 'typo', ie a typing error or misprint.

Litho Printing: Short for lithographic. Today's standard printing process, this works on the principle of greasy ink not sticking to those parts of the wet plate which are not to be printed.

Logo: Short for logotype. An identifying symbol or trademark; for example, Attic Press's logo is a woman pushing a pencil.

Make-up: The making-up into page of typeset material.

Margins: Areas of white space left around printed matter on page.

Mark up: To prepare a typescript for the typesetter by writing in the instructions such as type specification, width of setting, indentations, space between paragraphs and so on.

Masking: Covering the unwanted areas at the edge of an illustrations such as a photograph.

Mass market: Usually general-interest paperbacks, printed in very large quantities, aimed at a broadly-based market.

Matt: as distinct from glossy or dull finish.

Measure: The width to which a complete line of type is set usually expressed in 12 pt ems (or picas).

Megabyte: (Mb) One million computer bytes. Loosely means one million characters of continuous text, in storage terms, equals 150,000 words or two average-length novels 20 Mb = 3,000,000 words 50 Mb = 7,500,000 words.

Megahertz: Mhz refers to speed. Most micros are ruled between 5-20 Mhz.

Memory: Internal storage of a computer.

Menu: List of optional procedures displayed at start of a programme on computer screen.

Merge: Combine two or more files into one.

Microcomputer: Small computer.

Microfiche: Sheet film containing a large number of pages of information, photographically reduced to very small size, and readable only with a microfiche reader.

Microfilm: Photographic film with greatly reduced image.

Misprint: Typographical error. See **Literal.**

Mock-up: A layout or rough of artwork. Also called a visual.

Monograph: Study of a single subject.

Moral rights: The right of the author to be identified as the Author (originator) of the Work. This statement now appears on the same page as the Copyright notice. *(see chapter 6 on Contracts)*

Ms: Manuscript. Typed copy for setting. Also typescript, copy.

MTA: (Minimum Terms Book Agreement): The Writers' Guild and its sister union, The Society of Authors, has drawn up a draft agreement which it is hoped will improve the relationship between author and publisher. *(see Appendix D)*

Negative: Film in which the image of the original is reversed - the dark area appears light and vice versa. See **Positive**.

Net book: A book with a fixed price ensuring that books are sold at the same price.

Net Book Agreement (NBA): An agreement, drawn up between publishers and booksellers, to sell books at the retail price set by the publisher. *(see chapter 2)*

Net price: The final price or sum to be paid; no further discount or allowances to be made.

Net profit: The surplus remaining after all direct and indirect costs involved in producing the book have been deducted. See **Gross Profit**.

Niche publishing: See **Specialist publishers**.

Oblong: Book bound at the shorter dimension also Landscape.

Oblique: See **Forward slash**.

On line: Computer language meaning connected direct to a central processing unit and communicating with it.

op. cit: Abbreviation of *opere citato*, 'in the work cited'.

Option: The promise which an author gives a publisher to allow her to have the first opportunity of considering the author's next book for publication.

Original: A photograph, drawing, etc. provided by the author as copy for an illustration, as distinct from a proof, etc.

Origination: The process involved in the reproduction of original material, including make-up, typesetting and platemaking stages.

Orphan: One of those offensive words used in the world of publishing when the last line of a page happens to be the first line of a paragraph, ie it should be on next page.

Out of focus: Blurred.

Out of print (O/P): When all copies are sold and the publisher has no plans to reprint.

Out of register: One or more colours out of alignment.

Out of stock (O/S): When there are no copies of book in a warehouse/country and publisher is planning to move stock or reprint.

Outright payment or sale: A one-time payment by a publisher to an author, usually taken to mean that the publisher is buying all rights, including copyright.

Overlay: Transparent covering over artwork containing

instructions or additional detail. Also transparent layers of print matter, when placed on top of each other, form a composite picture.

Over-run/overs: Type matter which does not fit the design and must be either cut or the letter and word spacing reduced to fit. Also used to describe copies of a book which are printed in excess of specified quantity ordered.

PA: The Publishers Association.

Packager: An entrepreneur who conceives, commissions and produces books which she then sells to publishers in various countries.

Page: One side of a leaf.

Pagination: Page numbering.

Pantone: Proprietary name of a widely used colour-matching system.

Parenthesis: Round brackets () to printers a 'bracket' is a square bracket [].

Pass for press: To authorise the final form of a publication for printing.

Paste-up: Taking the text and illustrations and pasting them into blank pages of a dummy to show printer the exact position required. See **Mock-up**.

PC: Personal Computer

Perfect binding: The most common binding for paperbacks. This is more expensive than saddle stitching (staples) but cheaper than sewing.

Period: An American term for Full stop.

Permissions: The rights grants to an author or publisher by the copyright holder or her representative to reproduce copyright material, normally for a fee.

Pica: Usually refers to size of typewriter face with 10 characters to the inch.

Piracy: The publication of a book without permission having been given by either the publisher or the author and without the payment of any fees.

PLR: See **Public Lending Right**.

PLS: See **Publishers Licensing Society**.

Point of sale: Refers to eye-catching promotional material to be displayed where purchases are made. Produced mainly for general 'trade' books, for example, posters, dumpbins, bookmarks, badges, etc.

Point size: Size of type indicated in points showing the unit of measurement used to describe type size, ie 10pt type or 36pt type.

Portrait: Format that resembles an upright oblong, ie taller than it is wide. Normal book format. See **Landscape.**

Positive: Image on film in which black and white areas correspond to those in the original, as distinct from negative where values are reversed.

pp: Pages

Preface: A personal note by the author, placed before the main text, usually explaining how she came to write the book - as distinct from Foreword.

Preamble: The first part of an agreement which identifies the parties to it and the subject of the agreement.

Prelims: The first or preliminary pages of a book including half-title, title page, imprint/technical page, acknowledgements, dedication, contents, etc, before the text begins.

Print run: Quantity of book printed at any one time.

Printing process: Most books are now printed by offset lithography. Letterpress, printing direct from type, used to be the standard method.

Pro forma invoice: An invoice which is sent out in advance and must be paid for before any books are sent.

Proof: A trial printed sheet or copy, made before the production run, for the purpose of checking. Becoming more unusual.

Proof-reading: Reading typescript for errors. There is a standard series of proof-reader's marks which should be made both beside the mistake and in the margin. Typesetter's errors should be noted in red, authors in black and publisher's in blue. (*see Appendix H*)

Proofs: These come in various forms. Galley proofs are long strips of paper on which long columns of print, not yet cut up into pages, appear. Paged galleys are also long strips of paper, but the columns of type have been split into pages. Other proofs, now more common with DTP, are those made up and split into pages looking like the paperback book and printed from a laser printer.

Publication date: Date usually refers to 'official' launch date and/or when books are in shops for sale.

Published price: The price of a book fixed and advertised by the publisher as the retail price. It is on the basis of this price that the booksellers take their discount.

Publishers Licensing Society: The organisation which represents publishers and their interests in the Copyright Licensing Agencyand which distributes to its members the monies due to them which result from the licensing of photocopying.

R+D: Research and Development.

Range right: (or Left) align type to right or left.

Ream: 500 sheets of paper.

Recto: The right hand page (with odd numbers). See **Verso**.

Register marks: Trim marks, usually a cross in a circle, appearing on original artwork on every page in exactly the same position so that when two or more pieces of artwork are superimposed there is an accurate register or focus in colour printing. If incorrectly placed the job is said to be 'out of register'.

Re-issue: A publication which has been out of print and is then re-published either by the original or by a new publisher.

Release date: Date on which stock is released from the publisher's warehouse for delivery to booksellers in time for the publication date.

Remainders: Unsold books which are discounted. After a period, usually a minimum of one year, if books have failed to sell the publisher has the right to sell off stocks. The author is given an opportunity to buy surplus stocks before they are disposed of to a remainder merchant, who then releases them to the public at very cheap prices, usually through special bookshops.

Rep: Refers to the sales representative who promotes publisher's list to the booktrade in a specific area.

Reprint: Subsequent printing of the first edition of a publication.

Reproduction fee: Fee paid for the right to reproduce an illustration.

Reserves against returns: The withholding of a proportion of royalties until it becomes certain that the books have been sold and will not be returned by the bookseller or wholesaler.

Retail: Books sold, at fixed (retail) price books sold direct to bookseller (retailer). See **Wholesaler**.

Returns: Unsold books returned by a bookseller to the publisher with the publisher's prior agreement.

Reverse out: To produce text as white or a pale colour 'reversed out' of a darker background colour, as opposed to the more usual practice of printing in dark ink on a pale background - effective in small doses.

Reversion: The return of rights to the author following the cancellation of the agreement.

Review copy: A book sent to media for reviewing.

Review slip: The enclosure sent with review copy of book. It usually includes details of title, author, ISBN, price and publication date, as well as a request for a copy of any review that appears.

Rights: The legal entitlement to publish a particular work. Permission is given by the copyright holder (usually the author) to reproduce the book. See **Foreign rights** and **Subsidiary rights**.

Roman: Upright type (not bold) as opposed to *Italic*.

Root directory: In computing the main or 'top' directory in structure.

Rough: A sketch or layout

Royalties: Payments made to an author for every book sold, usually calculated as a percentage of the published (retail) price for home sales or of the price received (net receipts) for overseas and wholesale sales. Before any royalties are paid the advance must have been earned.

R/P: Reprinting

Rule: A line (of specified thickness).

Run: See **Print run.**

Run on: To continue text without a paragraph or line break.

Run on (r/o) costs: The costs of continuing to print, normally expressed in 500-1000, copies of book after an initial stated print run is completed, ie the cost of printing 3,0000 plus r/o of 500 to 5,000 copies of book.

Running head: Headline or title repeated at the top of each page. Sometimes the title of a book or chapter is repeated on all pages.

Running order: List of the contents of work to guide the printer.

Saddle stitching: a method of binding pamphlets, catalogues and sometimes small books. Wire staples are used.

Sale or return: Booksellers and wholesalers take books on the understanding that if they have not been sold by a specified period, they may be returned to the publisher, at the same time paying for only those they have sold. This leaves the financial risk with the publisher.

School supplier: (also called educational contractor). A firm which seeks contracts from both school and local education authorities to supply books and other educational products.

Search and replace: The facility of a computer programme to find all examples of a word or group or words in a file and replace them with another.

Search fee: Fee charged for picture research service.

Second serial rights: The rights which cover the sale of material to a newspaper or magazine for publication after publication in book form. However many times the material is re-sold, each sale is still or second serial rights (not third etc). See **Serial Rights.**

Serial Rights: Covers the sale of material, which range from the whole book to a single short extract, or any article or short story to a newspaper or magazine. The word 'serial' does not necessarily imply a series of instalments in succeeding issues of a journal, but can be taken in this context to mean 'newspaper or magazine'.

Serif; Sanserif: Serif is a typeface with 'handles' on the letters like most typefaces used in books, Sanserif means without 'handles'..

Sheets: When a book is printed the sheets have to be folded and collated before the book can be bound. Sometimes publishers keep part of the stock in unbound form (flat or folded and collated). These sheets (as opposed to bound stock) may be sold unbound, ie in co-edition deals or to a library supplier.

Show through: Amount of ink on one side of a printed sheet of paper which can be seen through on the other side.

Showcard: A point-of-sale, advertising and display card, set prominently on a counter or shelf in a bookshop.

(Sic): Used in written text to indicate that a surprising or dubious word, phrase, or fact is not a mistake and is to be read as it stands (sic).

Signature: When a printed sheet has been folded into pages it is called a 'signature'. Signatures usually consist of 16 or 32 pages (it is possible to have signatures of 4 or 8 pages). The extent of a book is usually a multiple of 32 or 16.

Soft copy: Non-paper version of text (ie, disc) as opposed to hard copy.

Software: Computer programmes.

Software package: A set of programmes written for a specific purpose, for example, word-processing (Wordperfect, Word5, etc).

Solid: Printed area with 100 per cent ink coverage or typeset with no leading between the lines.

Solidus: See **Forward slash**.

Specialist publishers: Sometimes referred to as 'niche' publishers, a publisher who specialises in a specific area, for example, medical textbooks, or feminist books, or for a specific group, for example, gay men.

Specs: Short for type specifications. Designers talk about 'doing the spec' by which they mean deciding text design. The specifications for printing a job are all the production details (format, extent, illustrations, print run, etc) sent to the printers for them to quote.

Spine: There are three sides to a book, front, back and spine. The look and design of a spine is becoming more important as books struggle for shelf space and 'front out' display.

Square Brackets: [] See **Parentheses**.

Stet: Ignore correction marked leave as originally set.

STM: Scientific, technical and medical publishing.

Stylesheets: Files or set of instructions that specify the design of printed or typeset output. See **Template**.

Sub heading: Secondary level of heading in chapter or text.

Sub-licences: When the publisher sells any of the rights of which the author has granted her the control, so called because they derive from the principal licence granted by the author.

Subs (Subscriptions): Orders for books secured from bookshops and wholesalers before publication date — the main activity of most reps. Their results are recorded by the publishing house as dues.

Subsidiary rights: All the rights which subside in a book, for example, translation, hardback, paperback, film, serialisation rights. Subsidiary Rights are sold by the originating publisher to a client for a negotiated fee, which might be an outright payment or as a royalty on sales.

Supplement: Additional part of a publication, giving extra (often late) information.

Swatch: Colour specimen print on paper or a set of such specimens.

Synopsis: Summary of complete contents of book usually prepared by the author in the hope that the publisher will read it.

Teleordering: System for ordering books whereby a subscribing bookshop can order books via one central computer. Every 24 hours the orders are split, consolidated and distributed to relevant publishers to fill. Should now be faxed to speed up orders.

Template: A page design or grid into which text and graphics are placed. See **Stylesheet**.

Terms: The discount and other selling arrangements on which a publisher supplies stock to a bookseller or wholesaler. Terms vary according to the amount of stock taken and the status under which it is accepted.

Territories: The specified areas of the world in which the publisher is granted the right to sell her editions of the book and to sub-license others to exercise various rights. The territories may be restricted further by a reference to the language in which the rights are granted.

Text: The body of typesetting in a book as distinct from headings and display type.

Thesaurus: A book of systematically classified synonyms and antonyms.

Thread sewing: Conventional sewing of book in sections, usually for hardbacks. See **Perfect bound**.

Tint: A solid colour reduced in shade or tone by screening (dots). Specified as a percentage of the solid colour.

Title: Publishers use this word as a synonym for 'book', ie we publish 20 titles per annum.

Title page: Page of a book carrying the title, author's name and publisher's name. Always a recto (right page).

Tone: Colour variation or shade of grey as distinct from Line which is solid black.

Trade discount: The discount given by publishers to retail and wholesaler booksellers on the price of book. The amount of discount given usually varies according to the amount of stock taken.

Trade paperback: Can mean a paperback edition produced from hardback edition using the same type therefore in large format. The paper is probably of lesser quality and likely to be perfect bound rather than sewn. It is not usually intended for the mass market so the price falls between that of the hardback and an ordinary paperback.

Trade publishers: Publishers of general interest books, usually mass market oriented.

Translation rights: The rights which cover the sale of the book to a foreign language publisher who will publish it in a version which has been translated into her own language.

Transparency: Also known as a tranny. A full-colour photographic positive on transparent film. Suitable as copy for separation.

Transpose (trs): Exchange the position of words, letters or lines, especially on a proof.

Trim: Abbreviation for 'trimmed size' of a printed piece of paper, ie its final or guillotined size. Trim marks alternative for crop marks.

Turnover: The total sales invoice value over a specified period for a particular company.

Type area: The area of final page size that will be occupied by type and illustrations, allowing for the blank border (white space) that will normally surround text.

Typeface: A specific style of type, eg Times, Helvetica, Palatino, used by publisher.

Typescript: Transcript. The hard copy (usually typed or a printout) of the manuscript or copy to be reproduced and printed. See **Ms**.

Typo: Short for typographical error, a mistake in the setting, introduced by the typesetter.

Typography: The art of designing type for printing or the arrangement or general appearance of typematter.

Uncoated paper: Paper with no coating and therefore not suitable for high quality illustrated or art work.

Unearned advance: The amount by which an author's total royalty earnings for a book fall short of the advance she received.

Unjustified: Typesetting with even spacing, therefore having a ragged right edge. See **Justified**.

Update: Edit a file by adding current data.

Upper and lower case: Upper case (U/c) characters are capitals, as opposed to lower case (l/c).

Upright: Format in which the head to tail dimension is greater than the width dimension (ie the normal book format. See **Portrait**.

Varnish: See **Lamination**.

Virus: An unauthorised programmed code introduced into an operating system so that when a (unknown) command is activated, the virus will corrupt the system and files.

Verso: Left hand page (with even numbers). See **Recto**.

Visual: A layout or rough of artwork also **Mock-up**.

Volume: Term meaning a bound book or used to express thickness of paper.

Volume rights: A vague term open to various interpretations. It usually means the right offered or granted to a publisher to produce the work in book form, plus the right to issue bookclub, paperback and other reprint editions or to license others to do so.

Warranty: The commitment that an author makes and which the original publisher may pass on to any sub-licensees that her material is original, does not infringe anyone else's copyright, and does not include anything harmful or in any way unlawful.

Weight of paper: Paper is sold in varying weights defined in gsm or g/m2. (grams)

White line: Line of space on phototypesetting.

White out: See **Reverse out**.

White space: Blank areas on a page.

Wholesaler: A person or company that buys books in bulk from publishers and resells them to bookshops and other retail outlets (ie newsagents) often securing higher than usual discounts in return for the large quantities taken.

Widow: or widow line. Highly offensive word emanating from the male-dominated world of publishing. It means a short line appearing as the first line of a new page.

Word break: Division of a word at a line ending.

Word count: The facility offered in some word-processing systems to keep a log of the number of words keyed in at any one time. Can also be done with spell checks.

Word-processing: The act of composing, inputting and editing text through a word-processor or computer or specific word-processing software.

Wordwrap: (or Wraparound) In word-processing, the automatic wrapping of text on to the next line when a line end is encountered.

Work: In most publishing agreements the book in question is referred to as 'the Work'.

World rights: May be expressed as 'all rights throughout the World' in which case there are clearly no restrictions on the publisher who is granted such rights. More often World rights are restricted in some way, for example, World Volume rights would not necessarily include many of the normal subsidiary rights, while World English language rights would clearly not allow the publisher to sell translation rights.

WP: Word-Process or Word-Processing.

WP format: In word-processing, a file format which contains all the printer control codes (soft carriage returns, etc) as opposed to an ASCII file format.

WYSIWYG: Acronym for what you see is what you get.

Appendix J

Selection of Awards, Bursaries, Prizes

Refer also to *Guide to Literary Prize, Grants and Awards in Britain and Ireland* compiled by Book Trust and *Writers' and Artists' Yearbook*

Arts Council of Great Britain: Write for full information on Bursaries, Awards, Travel Grants, Prizes.

Arts Council of Ireland/An Chomhairle Ealaion: Write for full information on Bursaries, Awards, Travel Grants, Prizes.

Arvon Foundation International Poetry Competition: £5,000 is awarded biennially for unpublished poems written in English.

Authors' Foundation: Grants worth £50,000, for research, travel and other expenditure to published authors working on their next book.

Betty Trask Awards: Annual prizes totalling £25,000 for authors under the age of 35 for a work of romance.

Book of the Year/Irish Children's Book Trust. Four prizes £1,500 to writer or illustrator of children's books.

Booker Prize: Annual prize of £20,000 for fiction written in English.

British Book Awards: Major categories include Author, Publisher, Bookseller, Children's Author and Illustrator of the year.

Christopher Ewart-Biggs Memorial Prize: Biennial prize of £4,000 for work which contributes most to peace and understanding in Ireland.

Cholmondeley Awards: Poetry awards worth £8,000.

Eleanor Farjeon Award: Prize of £750 for distinguished services by any person working with or for children through books.

European Literary Prize: Annual award of 20,000 ecus for work of any genre. Candidates must be nationals of EC country.

European Poetry Translation Prize: Prize of £500 given every two years for volume of poetry translated into English from a European language.

European Translation Prize: Annual award of 20,000 ecus for single work of any genre to citizen of EC.

Fawcett Book Prize: Annual award of £500 for fiction and non-fiction books which do must to illuminate women's position in society.

GPA Award: £50,000, every three years, for fiction or poetry by an author born in Ireland or an author resident in Ireland since 1989.

H H Wingate/Jewish Quarterly Prize: Prizes of £4,000, £3,000 and £1,000 for work which simulates an interest in of Jewish themes.

Ian St James Awards: Twelve annual awards to previously unpublished authors for short stories (5,000 - 10,000 words). Authors must be 18+.

International Poetry Competition: Prizes totalling £1,000 awarded biennially for best four poems, to anyone over 16 writing in English.

Irish Times/Aer Lingus Literary Prizes: Three annual prizes of £25,000, and two of £10,000 under three categories, for works of fiction in English or Irish published in Ireland, UK or USA.

Nobel Prize: Literature Prizes worth about £550,000 each for authors writing in English.

Shiva Naipaul Memorial Prize: £1,000 prize to writer under 35 for an essay (4,000) words describing a visit to a foreign place or people.

Kathleen Blundell Trust: Provides awards to published writers under the age of 40 to assist them with their next book.

McKitterick Prize: Annual award of £5,000 for first novels (published or unpublished) by authors over the age of 40.

Romantic Novelists' Association Award: Annual award of £5,000 for best romantic novel of the year.

Rooney Prize for Irish Literature: Annual award of £3,500 to Irish citizen whose work is published in either Irish or English and who is under 40 years of age.

Rose Mary Crawshay Prizes: For women, of any nationality, for work on any subject connected with English literature.

Rosemary Arthur Award: Annual £100 award for a first book of poetry.

Samuel Beckett Award: Two prizes of £1500 each awarded annually to residents of Ireland and Britain for stage or television play.

Stand Magazine Short Story Award: Prizes to value of £2,250 for an original, untranslated story in English not longer than 8,000 words.

T E Utley Memorial Fund Award: An annual award of £5,000 to a distinguished work of political commentary by a writer under 35.

Thomas Cook Travel Book Awards: Awards of £7,500 and £2,500 for books to encourage the art of travel writing.

Tom Gallon Trust: An award of £500 made biennially to fiction writer of limited means who has had at least one short story published.

Verity Bargate Award: Annual £1,000 for selected script.

Whitbread Literary Awards: A total of £30,500 under five categories. Writers must have lived in Ireland or Britain for three or more years.

Write A Story for Children Competition: Three annual prizes for an unpublished writer for a short story for children (1,000 words).

Appendix K

Reading List

Anderson, M D, *Book Indexing*, (revd edn) Cambridge: CUP, 1985

Article 19, Information, Freedom and Censorship: The Article 19 World Report, London: Longmans, 1988

Attic Press, *The Attic Press Guidebook and Diary*, 1993 (for list of groups). Dublin: Attic Press, 1992

Butcher, Judith, *Copy Editing*, Cambridge: CUP, 1981

Cashman, Aileen, *Money Matters*, Dublin: Attic Press, 1989

Cassell Directory of Publishing, London: Cassell/PA, 1993

Chester, Gail and Julienne Dickey, *Feminism and Censorship: The Current Debate*, Dorset: Prism Press, 1988

Clark, Charles (ed.), *Publishing Agreements*, (3rd edn), London: Unwin Hyman, 1988

Doubtfire, Dianne, *The Craft of Novel-Writing*, London: Allison & Busby, 1989

Fairfax, John and Joan Moat, *The Way to Write*, London: Elm Tree Books,

Fowler, H W, *Fowler's Modern English Usage*, Oxford: Oxford University Press, 1991

Gerrard, Nicci, *Into the Mainstream*, London: Pandora, 1989

Hart's Rules for Compositors and Readers, (39th edn), Oxford: Oxford University Press, 1983

Hines, John, *The Way to Write Non-fiction, Turning articles into books*, London: Hamish Hamilton,

Hoffman, Ann, *Research for Writers*, London: A&C Black,

Hyland, Paul, *Getting Into Poetry*, London: Bloodaxe Books,

Jones, Graham, *The Business of Freelancing*, London: BFP Books,

Journeyman Press, *Reviewing the Reviewers*, London: Journeyman Press, 1987

Kitchen, Paddy, *The Way to Write Novels*, London: Elmtree Tree Books,

Krailing, Tessa, *How to Write for Children*, London: Allison & Busby,

Lang, Kathy, *The Writers Guide to Desktop Publishing*, London: HBJ,

Legat, Michael, *An Author's Guide to Publishing*, London: Robert Hale, 1987

Legat, Michael, *Understanding Publishers' Contracts*, London: Robert Hale, 1992

Legat, Michael, *Writing for Pleasure and Profit*, London: Robert Hale, 1987

McNeill, Pearlie, *Because You Want to Write: A Guide to women and writing*, London: Scarlet Press, 1992

O'Connor, Joyce & Helen Ruddle, *Business Matters*, Dublin: Attic Press, 1990

Radice, Lisanne, *The Way to Write Crime Fiction*, London: Elm Tree Books,

Prone, Terry, *Write and get paid for it*, Dublin: Poolbeg, 1989

Russ, Joanna, How to Supress Women's Writing, London: The Women's Press, 1984

Sherry, Ruth, *Studying Women's Writing: An Introduction*, London: Edward Arnold, 1988

Small Press Yearbook, London: Small Press Group, 1992

Society of Authors, The (London), *Publishing Contracts; Quick Guides for Writers* and *What Price Reading?* (on NBA or support of retail price maintenance).

Stevens, Christopher, *Get Into Print: The Complete Guide to Self-Publishing*, Bristol: New Caxton Press, Flat Two, 11 Clifton Park, Clifton, Bristol BS8 3BX.

The Oxford Dictionary for Writers and Editors, Oxford: Oxford University Press, 1990

The Radical Bookseller Directory of Bookshops, Publishers and Periodicals, London: Radical Bookseller, 1992

Turner, Barry, *The Writer's Handbook*, London: Pan/Macmillan, 1991

Wells, Gordon, *The Successful Author's Handbook*, London: Pan/Macmillan, 1990

Writers' and Artists' Yearbook 1993, London: A&C Black, 1992

Trade Periodicals

The Author c/o The Society of Authors *(see Appendix A)*

Books Ireland 11 Newgrove Avenue, Dublin 4

Feminist Bookstore News 456 14th Street, Suite 6, San Francisco, CA 94103, USA

Poetry Ireland Review c/o Poetry Ireland, 44 Upr Mount Street, Dublin 2

Poetry Review 21 Earls Court Square, London SW5 9DE

Publishers Weekly PO Box 1979, Marion OH 43306-2079, USA

Publishing News 43 Museum Street, London WC1A 1LY

The Bookseller, Whitaker, 12 Dyott Street, London WC1A 1DF

The Radical Bookseller 265 Seven Sisters Road London N4 2DE

Index